Happy Mama

the guide to finding yourself again

Published by Affirm Press in 2016
28 Thistlethwaite Street, South Melbourne, VIC 3205
www.affirmpress.com.au

Text © Amy Taylor-Kabbaz 2016

Visit www.happymama.com.au

National Library of Australia Cataloguing-in-Publication entry available for
this title at www.nla.gov.au.
Title: Happy Mama/Amy Taylor-Kabbaz, author.
ISBN: 9781925344523 (paperback)

Design and illustration by Karen Wallis © Affirm Press
Layout by Jen O'Loughlin.

Cover photos by Jerusha Sutton
Cover design by Karen Wallis

Printed in China by 1010 printing

Happy Mama

the guide to finding yourself again

Amy Taylor-Kabbaz

AFFIRM press

For my babies Scarlett, Greta and Cass,
for all the mamas who have been brave
enough to share their journey with me
and for my own mama.

Contents

Introduction

There is a generation of mothers who feel as if they are coming last in every aspect of their lives.

Their days are filled with the heaviness of looking after everyone else. The concept of self-care or 'me time' feels like a luxury only celebrities and Instagram it-girls get to have. Massages. Green smoothies. Yoga mats. As the kids run wild in the playgrounds, these mums sit, flicking through images on their phones and feeling even more frumpy and forgotten. And so they give up.

They get to the end of the day, exhausted and aching. They turn the TV on to numb themselves with mindless entertainment. They know they should sleep – it's what they ache for all day – but if they don't use these night-time hours to do something even a little 'adult-like', they'll go mad.

It wasn't meant to be like this. Motherhood was meant to be a time of joy and chubby babies bouncing on our laps while we happily chatted with like-minded mamas in lush green parks.

We had expectations – and although we'd been warned about the lack of sleep and the death of our social lives, we didn't know it was going to be like *this*.

I know. I've felt that way. I've compared my life to all my social media idols and come out hating myself. I've felt bitter about other people's lives and angry that I've lost mine, and I've cried because I simply don't know how I'm going to get it all done. I've been there. And I've listened and nodded along as hundreds of mamas shared these experiences with me.

What's the point? they ask, sobbing.

It's too big. I don't have the time, the energy, the money, the support. I collapse at the end of the day and I'm awake all night.

I'm just surviving. I can't possibly add anything more to my list.

I don't know who I am anymore.

I'm not the person I want to be.

Until something breaks. It's usually the body that we notice first – we seem to be able to run on broken minds much longer than broken bodies. It's the niggling cold that never goes away; exhaustion; adrenal fatigue. For me, it was my thyroid. And then when that didn't stop me, it was pre-term labour with my son that finally screamed loud enough for me to listen. Only when the body finally breaks do we start to take notice. We go to bed early. We get help. But while we know we need to rebuild our bodies after everything we've put them through, we fail to see the importance of our inner health. We miss our spirits altogether.

But let me tell you, those can break too. When you don't find ways to nurture your own intuition, wisdom, thoughts and inner spirit, these too crumble. You yell at your kids. You disconnect from your partner. You hate your job, and you don't believe in anything. You have no faith, no grace, no trust. And that is when you lose yourself.

Connection depletion

A few years ago, an Australian doctor came up with the phrase 'postnatal depletion'. After years of seeing exhausted, rundown and sick mothers in his clinic – and watching the same decline in his own wife's health – Dr Serrallach coined the term 'postnatal depletion' to describe the physical health consequences of pregnancy and childbirth: lethargy, low immune systems, memory disturbances and poor gut health. Something that, he said, can affect a mama up to ten years after she gives birth.

Then Gwyneth Paltrow's website *Goop* posted about postnatal depletion, and it went viral. Suddenly people were talking differently about women's health after babies; books and blogs were written, and wholefood recipes were created. Which is all very good if you have the time, energy and enthusiasm for that. But in amongst all the hype, there was one part of this depletion phenomenon which, I believe, no one was really addressing. A part that, in my own experience, was even more important than the physical problems. I call it 'connection depletion'.

Connection depletion is our disconnection from who we are once we throw ourselves into being mamas. It's the complete lack of thinking about what we need because we're too busy juggling what everyone else needs. It's the global phenomenon of putting ourselves last. The good news? Reconnection can be done. The brilliant news? It's not as big a task as you think.

I want to make one thing clear: this book is not about the act of mothering. It is not about sleeping, discipline, routines, attachment versus helicopter versus abandonment. I am also not concerned with how you became a mama. I am not concerned with whether your baby was conceived on your honeymoon, on the couch or in a test tube. I am not concerned with whether you gave birth on the bathroom floor or in an operating theatre. And I am not concerned with whether you have one baby or six, whether you left a kick-arse career to have a child or whether all you ever wanted was to be a mama. I am concerned about you. I am here to speak to the woman who has entered the world of parenthood and is searching for a way to balance who she used to be with who she is now.

Please know you are not alone. No matter how you got here, we are in this together.

After the birth of my first daughter in 2007, everything changed. As a successful, career-driven and feisty gal, I was pretty sure I'd have this motherhood gig nailed. How wrong I was. My journey through motherhood has brought me to my knees so many times, and ripped me open to the biggest lessons of my life.

I have shed too many tears of anger, bitterness and 'what about *me*?' – and I know many of you have too. Being a mother really is a blessing, but only if we can also find ourselves on the way. No more putting ourselves on hold. No more spending every minute focusing on everyone else. Yes, this is about putting *us* first! 'First?' I hear you gasp? Yes, first.

A 2004 Australian study about children's views on work and family found that it didn't matter to a child how many hours their mother was away from home working; what mattered was how she *felt* about that work. 'To work or not to work is not the question,' said Barbara Pocock, the chief author of the study. 'The important question is not whether parents go to work but the state in which they come home.' It was how that mother felt when she walked through the door at the end of the day that had the biggest impact on her child's wellbeing. The kids payed far more attention to their parents' moods than to their work hours. If you're happy with how you are spending your day, your kids benefit. If you're stressed, angry or frustrated, they notice.

It's time for us to stop focusing on working or stay-at-home, home-schooled or day care: our only focus should be how every mama feels about her choices. How empowered she feels in what she is doing: whether it is a day of Play-Doh or an hour of paid work. So how do you feel about your choices?

The choice to take care of yourself

I've struggled with these ideas over the years. I've felt guilty putting my children into day care so I could chase my ambitions, and I've worried about their wellbeing when I've left them with their grandparents so I could go on a date with my husband. There was a fantastic book written a few years ago by Australian writer Karen Andrews called *Crying in the Car: Reflections on Life and Motherhood.* One morning after dropping her kids off, Andrews silently sat in her car crying over the angst she felt about juggling it all. Then she looked up and noticed other women doing exactly the same thing inside their own cars.

There are too many of us crying. As Arianna Huffington – one of the most influential women in the world – explains in her book *Thrive*, we need to redefine what it means to be successful, and crying in our cars should not be part of it. 'Every conversation I had seemed to eventually come around to the same dilemmas we are all facing,' Huffington writes. 'The stress of over-busyness, overworking, over-connecting on social media, and under-connecting with ourselves and with one another. The space, the gaps, the pauses, the silence – those things that allow us to regenerate and recharge – had all but disappeared in my own life and in the lives of so many I knew.'

Here's the truth: motherhood is the greatest gift to our generation of modern women.

It gives us permission to step away from what we have valued and tune in to the wonders of life. It strips back all we have ever known and believed about ourselves, and it leaves us raw. A wonderful thing! Because it is only when we go back to basics that we finally begin to see how amazing we really are.

I have spent the past eight years interviewing some of the most inspiring women I know about how they look after themselves while being busy, successful, fantastic mums. I've spoken with doctors, yoga teachers, actors, authors, nutritionists and some just pretty brilliant mummies I've met along the way. And each of them has agreed on some key parts of this journey. Those key parts are what make up the six focuses of this book, and they are tools we can use to help us become the Happy Mamas we want to be.

And what is a Happy Mama? This is my description:

A Happy Mama is a woman who is confident in her role as a mother, is happy with her purpose in life, is truly connected to herself, is clear on what she needs, and is confident in getting that. Every single day.

It's time we changed the dialogue around motherhood. It's time that we questioned the idea that to be a good mum we need to always put our children first. It's time we stopped putting such expectations on ourselves, got honest about what we really need, dropped the guilt and put our own oxygen masks on.

So here we go.

'Spiritual growth is like childbirth. You dilate, then you contract. You dilate, then you contract again. As painful as it all feels, it's the necessary rhythm for reaching the ultimate goal of total openness.'

Marianne Williamson, A Woman's Worth

Chapter 1

The Birth

Something happens when we become mamas. At the very centre of our souls, and in every cell of our bodies, we change – and I don't mean that just metaphorically. Feel like you don't know who you are anymore? That's because you are a newborn too. You've changed. Physically, mentally, spiritually.

I know you know this, because you can feel it. The things you used to be passionate about are different, and the things you never even noticed before have suddenly become really important. New doubts have crept in, new questions have been raised. Life gets put into perspective.

It's also confusing as hell. What happened to that clear path you had planned out? And what about your relationships, your body, your place in the world? Nothing is the same, and that's a scary thing to navigate while you're also trying to figure out how the hell to get through each day.

There's also a lot more pressure on women these days to do and be everything. Be a mum *as well as* superwoman at work, supermodel at the gym, and superlover in bed. Hardly a week goes by without another study being released on work–life balance, the pressure mums feel to lose the baby weight or how our busy lives are messing up our kids.

So with all this external pressure to be everything to everyone, and the added bonus of sharing every minute of our lives on social media, is it any wonder that we have become totally disconnected from the power and wonder of just being a mum? Is it a surprise that the majority of us are feeling overwhelmed, tired and disconnected from the joy we first felt at the birth of our baby, and are now just getting through one day at a time?

The first moments

After the birth of my eldest child, Scarlett, in 2007, I stood at the window of the maternity ward believing that I was the most powerful woman on earth. Despite the birth itself being far from perfect, all I could think about was how amazing it was that I'd created and birthed a new life. It's no coincidence that my daughter is called Scarlett. Scarlett O'Hara was my ultimate hero when I was growing up: strong, independent and feisty as hell. And a day after giving birth, as I stood overlooking the Adelaide parklands in the middle of a scorching heatwave, *I* felt like my hero. I silently said to myself, *As god is my witness, I will never doubt myself again.* And I believed it.

Sure, the birth was a bit of a horror. I was totally unprepared for the realities of a posterior baby and days of pre-labour stop-start contractions, and when the real contractions kicked in just minutes after being induced, I was terrified. My mantra was, *I'm never doing this again, I can't do this,* stuck on repeat in my head – and I remember feeling very, very alone. Terrified of each coming contraction, and alone.

Hours later, with no feeling from my waist down, I finally pushed my beautiful baby out – in the most undignified experience of my life. Legs in stirrups, a room full of strangers and a suction cap stuck to my baby's head. But once she emerged and was placed on my chest, I didn't care. Those blue, blue eyes staring up at me changed me in an instant, and I was reborn.

It wasn't until weeks later, when I found myself re-telling the birth story over and over again, that I started to feel less empowered by the inclusion of an epidural, ventouse, stitches. The oxytocin surge had kept the realities at bay long enough for me to have my Scarlett O'Hara moment, and for the first hours of my daughter's life I'd glowed. It was only when I started to compare my birth to everyone else's, and to face the realities of life with a newborn, that my confidence began to crumble.

Scarlett wouldn't feed. She was born with congenital torticollis (a condition where her neck muscles and one side of her jaw didn't develop properly because she was too squished inside me), and turning her head to one side was excruciatingly painful for her. 'Severe breast rejection' is what the nurses named it. Nice. You can imagine what that did to my new-mama glow.

Like so many first-time mums, I had only thought about the birth and not what came afterwards. I had assumed that breastfeeding meant I put my baby to my boob … and it just happened.

When it didn't, I blamed myself. I was a mess. I couldn't breastfeed, and my baby was 'broken'. She needed daily physio for her neck and a cast on her foot, which also hadn't developed properly and was pushed up against her shin.

Over the coming months, I bounced from one 'expert' to the next, putting my faith in everyone else's opinions. I never stopped to listen to my own instincts, because I didn't think I had any. Every day for weeks I checked myself in as a day patient at the hospital, walking from my home to the ward in a haze and longing to just get there so I could get some help. While I was there, I felt safe – the midwives could settle my baby, and I could learn how to be a mother. But once I was home again, I was lost.

I constantly struggled with my internal voice, which was telling me that I was a failure. I cried and cried, and I lashed out at my husband, Marque, for his inability to fix it. Of course I adored my little girl, but I hated myself. And I often wondered whether I'd done the 'right thing' by having a baby. Would my life have been better without children?

With physiotherapy and the guidance of a brilliant lactation consultant, Scarlett grew strong and could eventually turn her head to feed. Our life started to settle down, but I had changed. I had completely lost confidence in myself. I was ashamed that I wasn't the mother I thought I should be, and I felt so much grief for the life I used to have – and the woman I used to be.

Why couldn't I do better? Why didn't I love it like everyone else did? And what if I never felt like myself again?

I'd always achieved anything I'd set out to achieve. As a naive and totally Japanese-illiterate fifteen-year-old, I had been on exchange to Japan and survived. Years later I decided I wanted to study at a Tokyo university for a year, and I made it happen. I wanted to be a journalist for the ABC, so I became a journalist for the ABC. There was nothing I could not do – or so I thought. But that's the thing about motherhood – it's not about control. In fact, it's often the first experience in our lives that has nothing to do with our willpower or ideas of success. And that scares the shit out of us.

Not that we admit that. Oh, no, we don't talk about the pain of those early days, weeks and months of parenthood. We hide behind the new-mum mask, only ever showing the world the Instagram-worthy photos, brushing off the exhaustion and fear in the hope that no one will judge us. We avoid the in-depth discussion of childbirth that many of us need to have before we can begin to heal, and we aren't honest about the sheer difficulty of early breastfeeding. We're never told that every woman in the world questions herself and her abilities, and we suffer in silence as we collect layer upon layer of guilt on our exhausted shoulders. Surely if we just tried harder, did more, gave more, *were* more, we'd be perfect, like everyone else?

But sharing our pain is not weak. It is not weak when we begin to truly understand and accept the reason behind the pain: we are changing. Our lives have forever altered, and there is a grieving process connected to that. There can be no growth without pain – as harsh as that sounds. When something changes form, there is a shedding of the old. That's physics. That's the reality.

Falling in love with motherhood

One day, when Scarlett was only a few weeks old, I remember feeling so scared that I called one of my closest soul sisters. Eliza was a few years ahead of me in the parenting world, and is one of the most honest and tell-it-like-it-is women I have ever met. Her heart is big, and she has an ability to say exactly the right thing at the right time (usually with astounding wit). So, with that anxiety about my new world closing in on me, I called her. And the words she shared with me that day changed me forever.

'Motherhood is not love at first sight, Amy. Sure, it's lust at first sight, and you know you've found the one, but you still have to fall in love.'

Bam. Truth bomb.

And after years of self-reflection and research, I've come to realise that it's the same with ourselves. We have to fall in love with this new role. The love of being a mother, of completely reprioritising our lives and giving up so much of our freedom and spontaneity, is not a head-over-heels kinda thing. We fall in lust with the *idea* of motherhood, and we are smitten with all the oxytocin inside us, but love is much slower than that.

Love is unconditional. Love is accepting that tough times are part of the whole experience. It's showing up every single freaking day, and never wavering from your commitment. That is true love – and no one, and I mean *no one*, feels like that from the very first second with the very first baby. So it's time to stop beating ourselves up about it. No more hiding your shame, or wishing you'd done it differently, or wondering who the hell you are. It's time to start reconnecting with yourself.

Since Scarlett's birth, I have been falling in love with my true self. In hindsight I can see I never really knew myself before. I thought I did. But the reality is, it has only been through the years of births, babies and toddlers that I have glimpsed who I am at my core.

Before I could fall in love with myself, I had to respect myself, and as someone who had always been so driven, I had to ask myself what success was going to look like now. We've been told since we were little girls that success is being everything to everyone: the wife, the mother, the daughter, the sister, the colleague. None of which actually has anything to do with who we really are and what we really want. And ever since they first put our babies on our chests, we haven't had a chance to pause and reflect. We haven't even been able to have a shower without being interrupted, let alone figure out what it is we are lacking.

We have to redefine success. If we are to be happy with this time in our lives, we first have to sit down and figure out what it actually is that makes us happy. What does a good day look like to you? What lights you up? What soothes your depleted spirit? Who are you without all those material things you used to be attached to? How can you love the new you while still being the best mama you can be?

And ever since they placed that baby on my chest, I have been searching for the answers to those questions. How can I be happy giving my family everything they need, while still giving myself what I need? How can I love it all?

'When I made the changes
I knew I ought to make,
and followed my personal
commandment to "Be Gretchen",
I was able to change my life
without changing my life.'

Gretchen Rubin, Happier at Home

Chapter  2

The Search

I used to get the most terrible Sunday Blues.

Two years after my Scarlett O'Hara moment at that hospital window when I'd felt so proud and strong, I'd given birth to another little girl: Greta. That birth was a much more empowering experience, and Greta came into the world ready to bring joy. We called her Happy Boombi, and all she did was giggle. Within nine months, though, I was back at my old job with ABC Radio in Adelaide, and less than a year later, we'd packed up the family and moved to the Inner West of Sydney for Marque's work. When I resigned from my role in Adelaide,

I had visions of doing something different in Sydney – no more breakfast hours: I wanted something new after all my years in radio. But the buzz of Australia's largest city was contagious, and despite all my ideals of going at a different pace, I quickly fell back into the superwoman mode that has dogged me all my life. When the ABC in Sydney approached me just weeks after my arrival, my ego couldn't say no.

Within months, I was working on one of the top-rating breakfast radio shows in Sydney, getting up at 3.30am every single day to go to work in the pitch black. Breaking news and local stories, and making sure the presenter was happy, informed and ready. It was one of the best jobs in radio-land, and one I could only have dreamed of a few short years before. But I was struggling.

I was reminded of the film *The Devil Wears Prada*, and the line everyone kept telling Anne Hathaway's character, as she faced the harsh realities of her coveted position at a top fashion magazine: 'A million girls would kill for that job.' A million journalists and producers would have killed for my job, but all I could think about was throwing it all in and getting some freaking sleep.

For years, I missed waking my girls up in the morning. I missed getting them dressed, sorting out their breakfast requests and kissing them goodbye at the day care or school door. Breakfast radio hours did mean that I was always there for the 3pm school bell, but I was so exhausted, I felt like I was moving through a fog. My husband was working in the Sydney advertising world (think *Mad Men* without the perks) and was never home before 9pm. We were like two solo parents at either end of the day, and there were weeks when we didn't see each other from Monday to Thursday. But I just couldn't see past my daily alarm clock: the kids' bedtime was my bedtime, and if they weren't asleep and quiet by 7.05pm, Mean Mummy would come out. Again. But it was the job a million girls would kill for.

Sundays were the worst. My mum used to call them the Sunday Blues, and the women in our family seem to get them bad. A hereditary thing, perhaps, passed down in our super-sensitive DNA. There seems to be something about the end of the weekend that has us in tears. And so, one Sunday night, I decided that I needed something, anything, to refocus my mind on the positive week ahead, instead of all the early starts and missing out on my kids. And my first blog was born.

A new approach

Four years on, the lessons I had started learning after Scarlett's traumatic early months hadn't really sunk in – which I've found happens a lot on this journey. We learn something, get our big 'aha' moments, think everything will be different … until life gets in the way again. The kids get sick, the parents come to stay, Christmas madness begins. We're great at sticking to our plans for happiness when times are easy, but the second we get overwhelmed, it's back to the old patterns. And despite reading all the books on positive thinking and affirmations, I was still not really doing the work. Until that Sunday night when I thought, *I'll create a blog to get me through the week.*

I had been deeply moved when I first read Elizabeth Gilbert's *Eat, Pray, Love* – along with twelve million other readers. It was back when I was a first-time mum who was housebound and shit-scared about my new role, and the idea of running away to find myself in Italy, India and Bali was like morphine for my aching soul.

I longed to have my own little *Eat, Pray, Love* awakening – without abandoning my family.

So now that I had found myself back in that place of unhappiness, Liz Gilbert's story was big in my mind. I wanted my blog to be something like that – about my own search for myself. Then, as though a flash of inspiration was embodying me, I found it.

Seek, Act, Love: *Seek* out who you are now that you are a mummy, *Act* every day to connect with that woman, and *Love* your life.

My husband created my first logo, a colleague of his built the site, and I googled how to use WordPress. The excitement I felt over having a project outside of my alarm and a constant connection to Twitter was liberating, and it gave me renewed energy. The very first post I wrote was my first weekly 'Sunday Promise'.

I was always writing blog posts in my head, and I would rush home from my breakfast shift to squeeze in an hour of writing before school pick-up – even skipping the afternoon sleep to complete a new post.

It's astounding how small decisions change your life. I had no illusions about that blog being anything but a way for me to maintain my sanity. I was still fixed on the dream of being an ABC super producer and star, and I believed that such a traditional media organisation's response to my 'hippy' blog about being a mum would be complete ridicule. In fact, I didn't tell anyone at work what I was doing for a very long time. (Breaking out of that old self-judgement takes a while.) *Seek, Act, Love* did not cure me of my Mean Mama streak, or my disillusion with my career, or my addiction to busyness. But it was a start, and it did finally shift my thinking from 'poor me, my life sucks' to 'how can I turn this around so I can write about it?'

From there, I started to get freelance writing gigs, interviewing some of the brilliant thinkers and authors whose work I had been poring over at night. I remember sitting at my kitchen table one afternoon on the phone to Cheryl Richardson – a life coach and bestselling author specialising in self-care – heart pounding and thinking, *I can't believe I'm doing this.* I'd been working for the ABC for more than a decade at that time and had organised interviews with everyone from the Prime Minister to the winner of *Australian Idol* (who, just on the side, I was more flustered meeting than the PM), but to be speaking to Cheryl made me feel like I was watching someone else's life.

And it just kept flowing. Slowly, the blog grew. I started a Facebook page to support it and couldn't believe it when, one 3.30am start, I quietly checked the page and it had hit a thousand followers. Things were changing. I was commissioned to attend live events and write articles on Wayne Dyer and Deepak Chopra. Books would arrive on my doorstep with a note from a magazine or website editor asking, *Any chance you could read this then contact the author and do an article for us?* Healthy eating books, cookbooks, parenting books, financial freedom books: I did them all. And in every interview, I would have the motherhood angle in there somewhere. Always gathering information and insights for my small but growing tribe of readers.

But truthfully, I wasn't following my own advice. While I was blogging about the importance of self-care and writing about meditation, I wasn't doing any of it myself. I was pushing myself to do everything and be everything because I still hadn't accepted the lessons thrown at me after Scarlett's birth. I'd found the formula, but wasn't putting it into practice.

The superwoman complex

The trouble was that I still didn't value my role as a mother enough to slow down and listen. I had always aspired to the 'men's' jobs: I'd wanted to be a CEO, a journalist, a war correspondent. In my childhood imagination, there would be shoulder pads (it was the 1980s, after all), international flights, and rushing. Always rushing. Talking fast, walking fast, living fast. It's an image that a lot of the girls my age looked up to. So it's little wonder, really, that despite all that talk about slowing down, looking after yourself and letting go of the superwoman mentality, I had just kept on charging ahead in superwoman mode.

I used to get such a buzz out of people saying, 'I don't know how you do it.' It was like fuel for my insatiable ego, and so I would take on even more. Not even a surprise pregnancy with my little boy two years after starting my blog could slow me down. I still juggled everything, including my 3.30am alarm and solo parenting most days of the week. Whenever I felt overwhelmed, or insecure, or worried, I would go faster. Surely if I just worked harder and did *more*, things would be better? That's what I'd believed my whole life. That's the kind of role models I had.

As daughters of the feminist movement (whether you personally feel like you are or not), our generation is still trying to work out what womanhood means now. Our own mamas and grandmothers wanted so much for us. They fought so long and so hard for our rights to be doctors, lawyers and CEOs – and yet most of us were never taught how to be mamas, or were privy to the secret women's business that used to come from raising our families in close-knit communities. Mostly, we were taught how to climb the ladder, stand up against the boys, smash the glass ceiling. 'You can do whatever you put your mind to!'

Our world and our culture revolve around masculine energy: to-do lists, goals, promotions, striving. It's head stuff – not heart. And for many of the women in our generation, we've been all in our heads for most of our lives. Motherhood is not valued. Going slow and reading a book is for vacations (which are usually already peppered with guilt and constant checking of our phones). We don't know how to switch off, and we rarely pamper ourselves. Being successful is about *doing*, and not being.

But there's another way. Marianne Williamson calls it 'embracing Aphrodite'. It's accepting and nurturing our 'woman-ness' and feminine energy, and balancing it with the more masculine energy we have all been taught to worship. Aphrodite is our feminine energy, the goddess of beauty, sexuality, sensuality. She embraces her feminine power and relishes it, and somewhere over the course of the past few decades, we have disconnected from her.

How many of us are just so busy doing what we think we should do to be successful that we never pause to ask, 'Is this really success?' How many of us, like me, are so caught up in that old masculine, 'shoulder-pad' definition of success that we can't hear the niggling cries from our bodies and our spirits?

As Oprah says, if you don't hear the whispers, eventually the universe will scream at you. And scream the universe did.

'The wound is the place where
the light enters you.'

Rumi

Chapter 3

The Arrival

It was at my nineteen-week scan for my third baby that I began to see signs: what I was doing was just not working. My cervix was thinner than it should have been, the staff told me, and that could mean my baby would come early.

Being the pushy journalist, I questioned them about their data and statistics, but agreed to return in a week to check again. Seven days later, it had thinned another five centimetres. My cervix was not holding up to holding my baby in. I was prescribed progesterone cream to be inserted internally every night. I hated it and rejected the idea that there was anything wrong with me, but by twenty-four weeks it was obvious that the cream was not working. One afternoon straight after another long shift at the ABC, I went to the hospital for yet another internal scan and was met by the head of obstetrics. 'We think you need to stop work for four weeks,' he told me.

In a voice I imagined was usually used to disclose news much more serious than mine, he very calmly and clearly told me that my lifestyle was putting my baby at risk. 'It's obvious to us that your busy life is causing this thinning of your cervix – and because we can't change the fact that you have to look after two small children, we have to change your working conditions. You need to stop work for four weeks.'

My first reaction was, 'But it's a federal election, and I have to work!' I had proudly covered state and federal elections my whole career. They couldn't do it without me! But the doctor insisted. We just needed to get to the 'safe' mark of twenty-eight weeks, which was the absolute minimum gestation for a baby to survive out of the womb.

I'm ashamed to say I still rejected his advice. Yes, I stopped working – I burst into tears as I called my boss straight after the appointment. But I then spent three days trying to get a second opinion. I paid for a one-off appointment with the top obstetrician in Sydney, who, while not totally agreeing with my doctor, wouldn't risk telling me it wasn't necessary. I even called my midwife and cried to her about the injustice. Of course I was concerned about the health of my unborn baby, but I hated the idea that my body was letting me down. I hated the idea that I had failed.

Four weeks passed very slowly. I spent a lot of time writing my blog and coming up with grand plans for my maternity leave: I'd write an ebook, I'd run a course, I'd do this and this and this. I pitched more articles to magazines – and because I was doing it all from the comfort of my couch, I could justify my 'work'.

After exactly four weeks off, I walked back into ABC Breakfast Radio in the middle of the 2013 federal election campaign … and three days later I went into labour.

Breaking point

I remember the exact moment it all started to fall apart. I had just received an urgent email for the interview we were doing live on air – a last-minute press release or explanation or something 'breaking'. I hit print, jumped up, grabbed the paper off the printer and looked down at my belly. 'Hang on, buddy, we're going to run,' I said, and started running into the live studio to give the notes to the presenter. I think I even had heels on – always the professional (and a child of the 1980s), high heels were a prerequisite. Even when pregnant in the pre-dawn.

Just a few hours later, I started to feel funny. A weird pulling-down sensation began in my pelvis, and – I would only share this with a fellow mama – I started to feel the let-down sensation in my breasts at the same time. I'd never, ever felt this in my previous pregnancies, but I ignored it.

Over the next hour, though, I noticed the pulling-down sensation had a bit of a rhythm to it. *What the hell is that?* I thought. By that time I was all the way over the other side of Sydney, putting up posters with my three-year-old daughter for the workshop I was planning to run on postnatal support for new mothers (how ironic). But I decided to call the hospital – just in case – and of course they told me I'd better come in.

By the time we got to the hospital, I was having regular contractions. I walked up the hill to the entrance of the hospital with tears in my eyes, dragging my daughter alongside me as quickly as I could and pleading, *Please stay in there, baby. Please,*

please, please stay in there. I even started repeating it out loud as I rushed up the hill. 'Not now, little man. It's not the right time. *Please* stay in.'

They admitted me straight away and called Marque from work. Monitors were put all over my belly, and it was confirmed that I was having contractions. I was given medication to try slowing the contractions and steroid injections to strengthen our little boy's lungs for when he was born. Our only hope was that I would be able to keep him inside for twelve hours so I could have a second dose of steroids to help him breathe once he arrived.

The medication did seem to help, and things calmed down a little, so Marque went home to be with the girls and was told he'd be called if anything happened. The muscle relaxants I'd had made me drowsy, and the steroids had given me a terrible headache, so I dozed. But then, at about one in the morning, I was woken by contractions again – and this time they were really coming.

Every three minutes. Even the midwife said, 'Wow, they're really happening now.' Suddenly, my room was full. There was a visit from the neo-natal paediatrician, and the head of the department. The prognosis for a baby born at twenty-eight weeks wasn't the best – and we needed a fighter. We'd been playing around with a few names before then, but it suddenly became clear what our little boy would be called: Cassius. The first name of Muhammad Ali – our little fighter.

The contractions were certainly nothing like I'd had with the girls, but they were regular, and building. More medication was administered, and another dose of steroids. It worked. My uterus stopped contracting, and things slowed down again. My little boy was safe for the time being.

I spent five days in hospital to ensure that labour wouldn't start again. Five days during which I absolutely hit rock-bottom in my superwoman world. I couldn't ignore it anymore – my crazy-arse busy and ambitious life nearly brought our son into the world dangerously early. Enough was enough. Something had to change. If I could keep this baby in, there would be no more work, no more workshops and no more running between yoga class and school pick-up.

It was time to slow down and figure out a new way of being.

On that hospital bed, I downloaded my first ever chakra meditation – something I had been writing about and thinking about doing for months, but had always been 'too busy' to do. While focusing on each of the energy centres in my body and how to heal them, I had my first glimmer of awareness of how depleted my spirit really was. It felt completely empty. You would think that would have been overwhelming, but that meditation was something practical that I could latch on to, something tangible that I could start doing to help keep my baby inside. I also asked one of my girlfriends to bring me some notebooks, and I poured my heart out into those journals. *Why has this happened to me? What does this mean? Why have I been lying to myself and everyone else about how 'balanced' my life is? Why can't I be okay with just slowing down and being a mum?*

How am I going to be okay with slowing down and just being a mum?

Our generation of women have an addiction to busyness, and I was a junkie. I could not slow myself down or stop my ladder-climbing, even when my body screamed at me and I was screaming at my family. I could not slow my mind down long enough to be present with my girls when I was finally physically with them – I was always busy checking Twitter for breaking news so I could be on top of my job. I was looking for satisfaction and happiness in all the wrong places. Thank god, my cycle was finally coming to an end. My need for a daily 'fix' of busyness had been broken by sheer terror, and I was ready to rehabilitate. In whatever way I had to.

Cassius Kabbaz was finally born ten weeks later, at thirty-eight weeks. Labour began exactly three days after I stopped the daily progesterone and was told I could finally get off the couch. Three days of 'normal' life before my cervix let out. in a dark and quiet room in the birthing centre, with just my husband and a midwife, I caught my little boy's head as he entered this world. When I held him in my arms, I thanked him for already being my greatest teacher.

Becoming a Happy Mama

So, here I am. Eight years, two more children, and a hell of a lot of tears, tantrums and lessons – all of my own – since I first became a mama. I have trained as a postnatal yoga teacher and become an internationally accredited life coach, and I have read the best books and interviewed the best people I could find.

And I have worked with many, many mamas. Over 250 women, in fact – women who have also been desperate to start connecting to themselves, to stop feeling so lost and to start feeling happy again. Mamas who have connected with me on Skype for the very first time and burst into tears. Mamas who, as one client said to me, just longed to 'get their shine back'. But most importantly, I have lived this. I have made so many mistakes and promised myself so many things only to fall back into bad habits. I have been there, and I have clawed my way out.

The ideas and focuses in the next six chapters of this book have grown organically through those years, and are what I now believe make a Happy Mama.

When we're Happy Mamas, we stop yelling at our kids; we stop feeling like strangers to our partners and robots in our lives. We look in the mirror and like what we see, and we look at our homes and feel blessed with what we have. We find time in our days to breathe and reconnect, and we find ways to nourish our own needs along with those of our children.

One of the 'gurus' I have had the blessing to interview over the years is Caroline Myss. Caroline is one of the original leaders in the study of energy anatomy and the power of our thoughts, and as I spoke to her, I realised that what she was saying was finally bringing together all the 'bits' I had been trying to get my head around all these years:

'We've become far more focused on the role of organic vegetables than organic thought.' And there it is. We come full circle back to the connection depletion. It's time we paid attention to more than the food we are putting into our bodies, and realised the power of our thoughts. We have to start considering our spirits, our inner needs and desires as part of our lives.

How do we do that?

You start small, with simple daily practices to check back in with yourself. You start with your breath, and a few minutes each day. And you start to take on the ideas of kindness, strength, trust, grace, value and connection – the key elements I have come to believe add up to make a happy, mindful mama.

Kindness: because that's where it all begins: with a little kindness towards ourselves.

Strength: because we need to change the way we think about strength, and connect with how strong we already are.

Trust: because without it, we are lost.

Grace: because at the heart of it, this is what we are all longing for.

Value: because our role as a woman and a mother is far more valuable than we – or society – allow us to believe.

Connection: because we must build the connection to ourselves, our partners and the universe.

And finally, mindfulness. The ultimate destination. The ability to keep our thoughts in the present time, to stop the guilt trips and worrying, and actually be in the moment. No matter what.

In the following chapters, you'll find exercises to help you explore the focus a little more and make it practical. There are meditations, journal exercises, even some cleaning out of your wardrobe! Some of these activities may seem a bit 'out there' at first, but they work. The science is in, and it has unequivocally found that mindfulness and meditation have a direct effect on our brains, our hormones, our health and our happiness.

It is my hope that through these activities, stories and reflections, you will find your own way to bring these concepts into your life and discover how to be a Happy Mama. A mama who rides the wave of motherhood – the ups *and* the downs – knowing that she is doing the best she can. A mama who knows that happiness isn't about picture-perfect homes and perfectly mannered children, but a trust that she is doing a good job. That her happiness flows onto everyone else around her. And that she matters.

'Be gentle first with
yourself if you wish to be
gentle with others.'

Lama Yeshe

Chapter 4

Focus 1: Kindness

Oh my god, we are hard on ourselves.

Awful, mean, nasty. I have worked with mamas whose internal dialogues were so mean that they couldn't even say the words out loud. Judgement, hate, guilt. It's all there. And that's exactly why this whole journey must begin with kindness.

If there is one element that runs through every spiritual philosophy, every self-help book, and every yoga class I've ever attended, it's kindness, self-compassion, treating yourself gently. Being your own best friend.

Not that this is an easy thing to grasp. We compare ourselves to everyone else, we beat ourselves up for doing it 'wrong', and we home in on the bad bits with laser-sharp focus. And we are so very cruel in our judgements of ourselves.

Never before have we had to mother – and live – so publicly. Moments that in the past would have been very private are now willingly shared on social media, and even if you've decided not to be one of 'those' mamas, I bet you're still seeing everyone else's private moments, which makes you think about your own public image.

Have you ever found yourself viewing your children through the lens of Instagram? Or moved things around in your home before taking a picture so it's Facebook-worthy? It sounds crazy, doesn't it? This obsession with how people will view our inner world – and it's toxic.

We have lost the ability to listen to our own wisdom, and treat ourselves like we would our best friends. We go searching for anything that feels a little like connection – in the form of our phones and our social circles, but what we are really aching for is a connection to ourselves.

How do you speak to yourself? When you are quiet, and tune in to your inner dialogue, what are you telling yourself?

I know that you know compassion and kindness. I know because you are a mama, and you have felt deep, deep understanding and forgiveness for your little one when they have struggled. When they have been sick, or when they have hurt themselves, or when they've been just so over-tired they can't think straight and even the slightest change in their world causes a meltdown.

So you know compassion. Now you just need to turn that around to shine back on yourself. As the Buddha said, 'If your compassion does not include yourself, then you are not complete.'

Self-compassion is about looking upon yourself as you would your child or a loved one, and treating yourself in the same way. Dr Kristin Neff is a pioneer in researching and teaching about self-compassion. This is how she describes it:

'Compassion has three basic components: noticing suffering, being kind and caring in response to that suffering, and then remembering imperfection is part of the human experience.'

Perfectionism

Our harsh judgement of ourselves is often closely tied to perfectionism. We expect so much of ourselves that when we fall short of our own high standards, we're certain we have failed. And boy do we have a lot of standards to meet: perfect house, perfect body, perfect children.

Take the humble children's birthday cake. I will be the first to admit cooking is not my forte – and I'm usually quite okay with that. But when it comes to my kids' birthdays, I have always insisted on making their cakes myself. Perhaps it's a working mother guilt thing – I'm not always at home, I haven't always cooked the best meals, but at least I make the cake myself. Even if it's lopsided.

Scarlett's fifth birthday cake was a princess castle – with uneven turrets.

Greta's third birthday cake was a number 3 with hair clips all over it (her request, not mine).

And my attempt at Scarlett's sixth birthday cake – a 'disco ball' no less! – with a three-week-old baby strapped to me in the middle of a blazing heatwave … that was the real low point. It looked more like a giant silver golf ball with ball bearings sliding down the side than anything out of Studio 54.

But each birthday, I try again. And each year, I totally stress myself out. Until Cass's first birthday, when it finally dawned on me that I had this all wrong.

It was a perfectly acceptable cake. A big blue number 1 with Peppa Pig and George figurines plonked in the middle. It was even gluten-free, so I'd won a couple of healthy brownie points. But it lacked a certain 'something' – the something that would have made it social-media worthy.

When the icing wouldn't go on smoothly, and the top of the number 1 came out crooked, I started getting really frustrated with myself. *Why do I do this each year? I'm so bad at this! This is so embarrassing. I can't let* [insert name of girlfriend who is a freaking genius when it comes to cake decorations] *see this! Oh, I give up.*

I cried. I got angry at my kids and my husband because, for reasons no one could understand but me, suddenly every move they made and crumb they dropped was another disaster on top of my catastrophe. I even contemplated reaching for the wine before the party began, I was just so stressed out.

Instead of enjoying the process of baking for my little man – my last baby and therefore my last ever first birthday cake – I spent the morning stressing out. I panicked that it didn't look right, or that I didn't have the right party food, or that the bathroom wasn't clean enough before my guests arrived. I did what I do every time and went into a comparisonitis tailspin. Until I took a step back and became aware of what I was doing.

Buddhists believe that perfectionism is a form of hunger – a hunger for approval, for validation, for attention, or for control. It's a hunger that we have gnawing away at us, and we feed it by fixating on that which satisfies that craving right then.

The birthday cake was my hunger for approval. My obsession about a clean house was my hunger for control. My desire for the seemingly perfect family was my hunger for validation as a mother.

When I first discovered that, it was one of those all-body goose-bump moments. Perfectionism is a form of hunger ... so what was I hungry for?

What are you hungry for?

Is your desire to be perfect the only way you know how to stand out and be seen? Is it the only way you can feel in control in a world otherwise filled with chaos? Is it your way of proving that what you're doing is important by getting a nod of approval from your partner when they come home at night?

Ask yourself what it is you are really hungry for. When we see that it is in fact approval, control or validation that we seek, we can stop beating ourselves up, telling ourselves that we have failed, or are 'bad', or are ruining our kids' lives because it's not perfect, and instead ask ourselves …

'How can I give *myself* more of what I crave?'

We have to start with loving and accepting ourselves exactly (yes, *exactly*) the way we are.

Looking back at the past eight years of motherhood, I can see one of the moments my life really began to change. My *Sliding Doors* moment. Scarlett was about three months old, and I was yet to be diagnosed with the hypothyroid condition called Hashimoto's Disease, though I was suffering from its effects on a daily basis: it left me feeling exhausted, always cold, with no appetite and even slurring my words. I was also knee-deep in comparisonitis and had surrendered all my power to other people's opinions.

And I could have stayed that way, if it weren't for one simple sentence. I'd read Louise Hay's *You Can Heal Your Life* – a book that explores the direct connection between your thoughts and emotions, and your health and happiness – when I was a messed-up teenager living overseas, and it had certainly resonated. So after I'd read everything I could find on parenting and baby-settling techniques, I found myself picking up my old copy of Louise's book one night and finding the single thing I really needed to hear as a mama:

'I love and accept myself unconditionally, right now.'

Of course I didn't believe it. I didn't accept any part of myself, thank you very much! But what truly transformed my whole world was Louise's suggestion that for twenty-eight days, you repeat this line to yourself whenever you think of it. You write it on a post-it note and stick it on the bathroom mirror. You tell yourself while you're cleaning your teeth, while you're driving the car – whenever.

So, in my under-active thyroid haze, I began. I repeated it over and over and over, using it as a mantra. I said it in time with my footsteps on the pavement as I pushed the pram every afternoon, and I repeated it to myself every time I felt like I couldn't cope. Eventually, a few days into it, I started really *hearing* the words.

I accept myself. Wow … I accept myself. Really? I accept myself. Unconditionally. No conditions … just the way I am … I accept myself.

I don't think I had ever fully accepted myself before. I had tried to be what I thought I should be – a brilliant journalist, the perfect best friend, the best sister, the ideal daughter – but it was always about changing myself into that person. It wasn't real acceptance. In fact, it wasn't even an honest view of who I was.

But accepting who we are and all our flaws, bumps and bad days is what this life is all about. Don't you want to finally just be okay with yourself? Aren't you sick and tired of trying so hard, only to fall short of your own high expectations of what you think you should be?

Don't be alarmed when you first tune in though – I was shocked when I started to listen to my thoughts! *I hate this, I can't do this today*, and *Oh my god – I'm such a bad mother*. And once I noticed it, I only beat myself up more. *Not only am I a bad mother, but I'm also a terrible person to myself!* Hello spiral pit of despair.

Please don't judge what you hear. Just as we know all too well that our body and health have a long way to go when we first walk into a gym, acknowledge that your thoughts have a long way to go when you first start paying attention to them. But we have to start somewhere.

Now whenever I start to feel anger or frustration or overwhelm creep into my day, I know to check in with my body and my mind. I tune in to what my inner Mean Mama is telling me (usually something along the lines of 'when is it my turn?' or 'why is this so hard?'), and I drop my shoulders, breathe, relax my throat muscles and smile to myself.

You're doing a great job, Amy. It's okay. Let it go.

I still have to keep working on it – just like we have to keep having healthy food day after day to reap the benefits. One chemical-free apple won't last a lifetime: one positive thought won't get you through a tough year. We've got to keep working on it.

As Eckhart Tolle says, 'What a liberation to realise that the voice in my head is not who I am.'

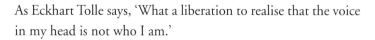

What is that voice telling yourself about you?

And what is the actual truth? Start by asking yourself:

♡ How do I feel about myself right now?

♡ How do I talk to myself, and treat myself?

♡ If my best friend in the world was saying these things about herself, what would I say to her?

♡ What do I know I'm great at?

♡ What am I proud of?

♡ What do I need to forgive myself for?

♡ I believe I am a good mother because …

♡ I believe I am a good person because …

And now, write yourself a little message. Something that you can come back to over and over again, whenever you need. A love note, of sorts.

Start with your name, and then, 'you are amazing, because ...'

A lot of the mamas I have done this exercise with have really struggled with these questions. The idea of reflecting on what we are really good at is too daunting – and only makes them feel less adequate when they realise they don't feel very proud of many things anymore. But what I find is that most of them are overlooking the most basic (and important) things they are already doing.

Like cuddles. Like knowing how to comfort a sick child. Like baking muffins, singing in the car, being a supportive friend, or remembering people's birthdays. Putting others first!

One mama once sent me an email outlining all the things she thought she was doing wrong and all the ways she was failing as a mother and wife. She told me that she could hardly see the screen, she was crying so much – she just felt lost and desperate to change.

After pointing out that she was amazing to even be declaring that enough was enough and it was time to change, I asked her to send me back her answers to those questions. 'I know it's hard,' I told her. 'But start with the smallest things.'

This was her response:

I'm finding it really hard to find things that I'm 'great' at and that I 'like' about myself, but –

♡ I'm great at reading books to my girls. I'm quite animated in my delivery and it's enjoyable for us all.

♡ I'm good at encouraging and supporting others.

♡ I'm good at verbalising my feelings.

♡ I'm good at handstands.

♡ I'm good at finding things in the dark – if something has been dropped, I can find it.

♡ I'm good at hearing a noise in the middle of the night and determining where it came from.

And that is what it's all about.

Every time that mama finds something in the dark, or reads to her children in a big bear voice, or does a handstand, she's going to reflect on this. She's going to feel stronger and prouder. She's going to know that this is her special thing for her family – and start to feel better about herself.

Find the small things and go from there. Some of those negative mantras have been embedded in our brains for most of our lives. They are the words we've been listening to for decades: a bad earworm that is on repeat day in and day out. So don't be hard on yourself if your default mantra is pretty mean.

If you catch the negativity on high rotation in your mind, simply start by giving it a little wave and saying, 'Hi. I know you. But I don't believe you anymore.'

As Pam Grout so perfectly explains in her fantastic book *E-Squared*, changing our thoughts is like toilet-training a puppy: every time we find the puppy peeing behind the couch, we pick it up and take it outside to the tree. Pick it up, and show it the tree. Over and over again. And one day, the puppy will just go to the tree.

Our thoughts are no different. Pick them up, and show them the tree. Before we know it, they'll wander out to that tree all on their own.

Kindness Techniques:

A GRATITUDE DIARY

Repeating affirmations can be great, but when we first start to tune in to our thoughts and the stories we are telling ourselves, it can feel like a big (fake) leap of faith to turn that thought of 'I can't do this anymore' into 'I love my life'. *Big* leap of faith.

So, what do you do?

You may have heard of a gratitude journal – a diary that records what you are grateful for that day in the hope that like attracts like, and the more positivity you focus on, the more you find to be thankful for! Maybe, like me, you've even dabbled in the practice at times. I'd had an on-again-off-again relationship with it myself, until I read this quote by Ms Oprah Winfrey in her book, *What I Know For Sure*: 'Sometimes we get so focused on the difficulty of the climb that we lose sight of being grateful for simply having a mountain to climb.'

Oh, that sentence. That gets me every single time. I don't know about you, but I want to feel that. I want to feel that, every single day. I want to see the challenges as my mountains, but ones that I know I can climb to reach greater heights.

Start being grateful for your climb. Start reflecting every day on what you are thankful for – whether it's in an electronic diary (just search on Google), which allows you to make notes on what you're grateful for as you go about your day, or whether it's on good ol' paper. Make it a habit – like your coffee or your shower. Start by listing five things that you are thankful for that day, and try to mix them up a bit.

While it's lovely to be grateful for your kids every night, that's really not the point. What we're trying to do here is find the good in the bad, the blessing in the tough; that way, you can start reprogramming your inner Mean Mama to be a little kinder. Even if at the end of a struggle day all you can think of is gratitude that everyone is finally asleep, you have a clean soft bed, your warm cup of herbal tea and the ability to get up in the morning and try again. Make it a part of your day, and climb that mountain.

CREATE A SPACE IN YOUR HOME THAT IS YOUR SANCTUARY

Kids' toys, folded laundry, busy little people all around us: our homes are not always the sanctuaries we wish them to be. That's okay – that's our reality right now. But having our own space in which we can retreat, connect, take a few big breaths and feel like ourselves again is very, very important. Especially when we're feeling completely over it.

Is there a space in your home that you can call your own? Can you set up a little 'altar' to your self-care?

Mine is my bedside table. That's the only space I can find right now, but that's alright. I have my affirmation cards, a few crystals, a candle, hand cream, my favourite books and my journal. And when I sit down on my bed, whether it's in the middle of the day to sneak in my three-minute mindful meditation, or at the end of a very long day, I breathe differently.

It is my space. It's a place where I can be okay with just focusing on the moment.

Create a little space for yourself. What can you bring into it to make it feel sacred? How can you honour the woman you are, and the work you are doing on yourself right now?

Inspiring Interview:

Sarah Napthali

Sarah Napthali is one of the most inspiring mamas I've ever met. Her books on Buddhism and motherhood changed not only my life, but the lives of thousands and thousands of mamas around the world. So you can imagine how excited (and nervous!) I was when I first reached out to her and asked if she'd share some of her insights into how motherhood is one of our greatest spiritual practices. And then she said yes! Here are some of her beautiful thoughts on self-compassion, kindness and turning housework into meditation practice.

Motherhood is an amazing opportunity to start to ask yourself the big questions in life: like who am I, and what does this all mean? When you become a mother you might feel like you're taking all these steps backwards. Backwards in your career, backwards in your income, backwards in your social life. But if you're on a Buddhist path, then you're actually taking many, many steps forward and learning about really important things like impermanence, and that you can't hold on to anything because change is the only constant.

I first came to Buddhism when I was twenty-four, and I found a book called *The Heart of Buddhism* – which I just loved. I probably read it once every year for about six years. But I was only sort of flirting with Buddhism at that point and incorporating it into my life on a very ad-hoc basis.

I think I had an epiphany when I was pregnant – or maybe a series of epiphanies, I can't remember anymore – but I thought, 'I really want to be on a good course for this motherhood thing.' I'm not sure if I had faith in myself to do this very important work of motherhood. I had made lots of silly decisions in my past, and I wanted to put myself on a path where there were mechanisms to keep me on the straight and narrow, so I wouldn't fall into depression or neuroticism or anger or self-pity or all the different things that we're all prone to. And I just thought, 'Look, Buddhism provides all these tools. I am really going to ramp up my practice and get much more serious about meditating. I am trying to live mindfully, I am trying to be compassionate about all the people in my life.' So being pregnant with that first baby was a very big step on the path.

When a woman becomes a mother, it's potentially a very stressful time. Everything she thought she was, and all the things that gave her life structure are ripped out from under her. She is faced with isolation, she's at the beck and call of her baby or she's got toddlers interrupting every conversation – or in my case, I had a toddler who was always running away, and it felt like I was just chasing him for a couple of years. At social gatherings I couldn't even participate because I was always running!

There can be a lot of frustration at all the drudgery, and we can get into the habit of believing our thoughts and letting them push us around rather than saying, 'That's just a thought, it's not the truth. It's just this crappy language that's passed through my head and it's really nothing.' You know most of it is rubbish, most of it's kind of grumbly, it's all self-centred and it's often deluded.

Mindfulness and meditation [which are central to Buddhist practice] are about learning the skills to watch your thoughts and feelings. You develop this capacity to watch it all come up and not identify with it quite so much, which in turn has an effect on the way you behave, the way you talk, the way you think. And as time goes on, you just see yourself growing and maturing because you've become more aware of the ways you sabotage yourself and sabotage your happiness.

One of the ways we can start tuning into our thoughts is actually through the housework: the washing, the folding, the sweeping.

That's what happens in Zen monasteries and on Buddhist retreats – there's always some work to do. Everyone's on a roster and you practise doing these things mindfully and watching the thoughts that come up.

And some of the thoughts that come up are very grumbly. *Why am I doing so much of this? My husband should be doing more of this. My kids should be doing more of this. Jeez, I hate this, I did this only yesterday, this is never-ending.* But if we try to do the work mindfully, we realise that the way we label housework as 'menial', 'inferior' and 'boring' affects our attitude towards it. I don't want to be a total hypocrite here, because I can get as grumbly about the housework as the next person – even after years of practice. But tuning in to how we think about it is a big first step.

It can be a bit dangerous when you first start watching your thoughts, and you're actually shocked by how self-absorbed you are or how mean you are or how angry or cranky you are. You could start to really hate yourself, and then you start meditating just to change who you are.

But you've got to meditate from a place of self-acceptance. I accept myself, I love myself – warts and all. And if you've got that attitude then you've got the guts to look deeper. If you hate yourself then you're scared to look at the murky stuff that you're going to find. Self-compassion is definitely the real cornerstone of my practice. It's one of the very first things we need to learn as mothers and as women, because there's just so much potential for feelings of guilt and shame and inadequacy.

If you can apply the kind of compassion to yourself that you have for your children when they err, it's a good way of pressing the accelerator on your practice. Mother the mother. Take inspiration from that unconditional love you have for your children. You can forgive them anything and you can get over anything they have done – you can do that for yourself as well.

Sometimes I actually do it physically. I just take my right hand and give my left arm a little rub – the way you comfort a child who's upset. That sort of human touch releases oxytocin in the brain. If I am in a meeting or at work and I can't give my arm a rub because I'll look like a weirdo, then I can do it mentally, and I don't think the brain knows any different. You can get that little oxytocin boost whether you do it mentally or physically or sitting in meditation. Just think about giving yourself a hug or a rub, or some kind of reassurance that you'd give a small, vulnerable child.

'The gateways to wisdom and learning are always open, and more and more I am choosing to walk through them. Barriers, blocks, obstacles, and problems are personal teachers giving me the opportunity to move out of the past and into the Totality of Possibilities.'

Louise Hay

Chapter 5

Focus 2: Strength

I spent years of my life believing I wasn't very strong. I would set goals and promise myself that I'd never do something again ... only to give up and give in. I have diary upon diary from my teenage years filled with 'from tomorrow onwards I will not ...' followed by another entry beating myself up that I didn't stick to what I'd said. I equated willpower with strength, and therefore thought I didn't have any of either.

How wrong I was. True strength doesn't come from willpower. True strength comes from the ability to dig deep and keep on going. It's the way you put others first when they really need it. It's the times you have amazed yourself with what you can achieve. That's what this chapter is all about.

When we start to connect to the idea of true strength, and how we always have it at our disposal, we start to view ourselves in a very different light. We start to see the warriors we really are. We start to connect to that inner goddess (yes, goddess) that is always there, waiting for us to call upon her.

The reason we don't believe we are strong is because we have the wrong definition of it. We think 'strong' means that woman who never yells, who is always solid and clear on what she needs to do and when. Or, I would argue, we actually don't even know *what* strength means to us.

I did not think I was strong as a mama. I didn't make it through labour without an epidural, I couldn't cope with the endless sleepless nights and I crumbled at the idea of spending day after day at home with an unhappy baby. I also believed that I wasn't strong because I couldn't say no to that extra glass of wine when I was out, always going too far and feeling so ashamed the next day.

Weak. No willpower. No determination.

And when I started to pay attention to my thoughts and finally tried to turn things around, I couldn't stick with it. I promised I'd meditate and didn't. I promised I'd put myself first, cut back on sugar, do more exercise and stop wasting money on crap that never made me feel any better … and I didn't.

So where was my strength?

The strength of being a mother

In our society's core belief system, strength is still considered a masculine quality. It's determination, commitment, solidness. It's climbing the ladder, smashing the walls in front of us and kicking goals. Once again, all masculine.

We don't value the strength it takes to nurse a child every three or four hours a night for months on end because a) we think we're crap at it, and b) no one says, 'Wow, look how strong that woman is, she is a mother.' Nor do we value the sheer tenacity and strength it takes to juggle so many other people's needs to the detriment of our own. Let's be honest here: my husband would not be able to do what I do. He does not know the first thing about what needs to be taken to school on which day, which bills are paid from which account or what the kids are going to get for their birthdays. I love my husband to death and he is the perfect guy for me, but most of the time, his children's birthdays come around as a bit of a surprise to him each year.

He can't do what I do. He just can't. But do I look at what I do every single day and say, 'Wow, girl, you are so strong to do all of this day in and day out'? Nope. Most of us don't.

I want to get something really, really clear (if I could stand up in front of you right now, I would – that's how important this is): you are strong *because* you are a mother.

You don't need any other evidence. You don't need to list 'How I got through this', or 'I know I am strong because …' (although, that does help silence the inner Mean Mama). All you need is to accept, on the deepest level possible, that you did it. You are doing it – the hardest job in the world. Nothing else makes you stronger.

Here's the thing that I think is the source of so much of our disconnection from our power and strength as women – and the source of so much pain. We have taken our power away from ourselves, often at the very beginning of our life as a mother.

Becoming a mother is meant to be the most sacred time in our lives. It's meant to be our connection to the divine feminine: that part of us that brings life into the world. We all have both a masculine and feminine energy within us, but thanks to society's celebration of the masculine way, we are not really supportive of the feminine. The softer, more sensual, more connected energy. Motherhood gives us that chance – it's a journey of soul-level spiritual awakening, when we begin to nurture another life. But modern-day motherhood is rarely that.

Pregnancy is over-managed. We are prodded and poked and measured and tested. We are disconnected from the wisdom and wonder of our body, and filled with fear and statistics. And what if we don't just fall pregnant naturally one lovely Sunday evening, when all the stars align? Then we have failed before we have even begun. There's something 'un-womanly' about us. We're broken.

Once again, our power is taken away. We disconnect from ourselves as women. We doubt ourselves.

Yet here we are: mothers – however we made it happen. Whether it was through test tubes and injections, caesareans and epidurals, we're here. We did it. Isn't it time to look at that as a win?

There are very few women in this world who are happy with the way they birthed their babies. Some just wish things could have been slightly different, while others hold a lot of pain and grief about the process. Our medical system has taken the life-changing and life-saving modern procedures that we desperately need in some circumstances, and turned them into something disempowering and invasive. Even when we need these miracle procedures to save us and our babies' lives, we don't feel empowered by that choice. We feel shamed, or sad, or like we failed.

Enough.

Enough with the judgement of how you did it and how she did it. Enough with the disempowerment of new mothers. The only difference between an empowering birth and a grief-ridden one is the mother's feelings of being heard and involved – that's where her strength comes from. And if she has that strength, my god, she can get through anything.

Finding empowerment

Let me tell you a story: when I was pregnant with my little boy, my sister was also pregnant a few months ahead of me, and she approached her birth preparation with the zest most new mamas do – a total dedication to having a divine, natural birthing process. She and her husband are very mind-over-matter kinda people, and they approach most things in life confident that they can make it happen. They did the Calmbirth course; they read the books. Her husband, a seriously competitive man who always needs a project to work on, viewed coaching my sister through labour as a personal challenge – there was no way they weren't going to go through it!

But as our children (and the universe in general) so often do, her little boy had other plans.

Her son was breech. And I mean, really, really happy to be wrong-side up, with his head close to his mama's heart. No matter what my sister did, this stubborn little guy would not budge – and boy did she try everything! There were two attempts at turning him, there was acupuncture, yoga and herbs. I think she and her husband single-handedly pushed the number of Google searches for 'how to turn a breech baby' to record numbers … but no. This bub wasn't moving, and their obstetrician believed that a caesarean birth was the only option.

This is the wonder of parenthood. For most of her life, my sister had gotten what she wanted: at university she was known as Teflon Woman because nothing bad ever stuck to her. She had always been blessed, most would say, and so this threw her. Why couldn't she get what she wanted?

It didn't help that I'd had a natural breech birth with Greta. Although it had been suggested I should also opt for a C-section, I found a midwife and obsetritician who supported my plea to 'just give it a go', and as it wasn't my first baby and she was in the perfect position, everything went to plan. But for my sister, my beautiful and empowering natural breech birth must have been like someone waving their best-in-class award in front of her nose, just moments after she discovered she'd failed. I was aware that any insights from me would only be pouring salt on her very tender wounds, so I backed off. This was her experience, and I tried to respect that.

Finally, after many tears of anger and fear, they gave up their dream of a natural birth and accepted their obstetrician's view that a caesarean was their only option.

She could have hung on to that anger and fear. She could have stayed in the 'woe is me' camp – and I don't think I would have blamed her. It wasn't fair that she couldn't get a go at it like I did, and it wasn't fair that a C-section with her first made a natural birth with her second less likely.

But do you know what my supremely capable and inspiring sister did? She totally empowered herself to make that birth the most natural version of a caesarean she could. She spent night and day researching the latest on the health of babies after C-sections. She had a trainee midwife with her to ensure their wishes were met. She had a meeting with the obstetrician about letting the cord blood run out until it stopped pulsing, and arranged for her husband to cut the cord. They organised for the baby to have skin on skin contact with both her and her husband in recovery. The midwife attending the birth said that she has never seen a caesarean like it.

The morning of the planned birth, my sister got up before dawn and filled her lounge room with candles, put on the birthing playlist she had put together for their dream natural birth, then sat on the floor and spoke to her unborn baby boy. She stayed there, preparing for his arrival and bonding with the process. At one stage her husband woke up and came down to find her there, and he joined her. They sat on that floor and had the natural bonding process they had dreamed of.

And then, just days after they came home from the hospital with their new baby, my sister ran a bath, got into it with her newborn son and lay in the water, 'giving birth' to him in her mind. She held him against her wet skin, and just lay there with him. Feeling him become a part of her.

You can't tell me that's not a deeply empowering and beautiful birthing story. And you can't tell me that my sister's approach to what could have been one of the biggest disappointments in her life is not a show of true strength and resilience.

So what is strength?

Strength is making a choice to pick yourself up and find a better way. Strength is knowing that there are going to be challenges and tough nights and times when you just want to scream (and maybe you will), but you get through it. You learn from it. You grow, you find your power again and you keep on going.

You have that strength. We all do. And if you can't see the power in your birth, or your time as a new mama – or not-so-new mama – you need to rewrite the story. It's time to talk to yourself as you would to your best friend, and point out all the ways you *didn't* crumble under the pressure, and remember just how resilient you are.

Try thinking about when you have shown that strength. Say to yourself, 'When I look back over my life, there have been times I have amazed myself with my strength in the face of adversity. When I have proven I can get through anything. These times are:

1 _____

2 _____

3 _____

4 _____

5 _____

(Yep, five. I know you can find them.)

Find those times and hang on to them. Be proud of them. Let them define you, so that next time Mean Mama kicks in with her negative 'you can't do this' voice, you've got a sassy answer for her. 'Oh, really? Well, I got through *that*, so actually, yes. I can.'

Strength Techniques:

 ACCEPT YOUR BIRTH

Not all of us have had a dream caesarean. Nor a great natural birth. Post-traumatic stress and grief after a difficult or out-of-your-power birth are very real, and can mean you start your life as a mum feeling completely disconnected from the actual *process* of becoming a mother.

In my experience, we can forgive ourselves and the people involved, and we can reclaim a little of that strength. It's painful and very emotional, but I have had dozens of mamas write to me after doing this exercise to say how much it helped them heal. I've had mamas say it changed the way they felt about their children and about their partners, or doctors, or people who let them down. And, most importantly, it finally allowed them to feel compassion towards themselves, and see that in the end the very fact that they *are* mothers is enough.

So here it is: If birth grief or disempowerment is something that is stopping you from feeling fully connected to yourself, please try answering these questions in the most gentle and self-loving way you can, and then follow the meditation. It is best if you can make this a little ceremony (think of my sister's moment on the floor with her planned birthing music and candles), or at least a time when you can really get into it.

Start by asking yourself (and journaling if you can), the answers to these questions:

♡ How do I feel about the birth? (If you have had more than one baby, it's really beneficial to do this separately for each birth.)

♡ Am I proud of the outcome?

♡ Do I feel empowered by the process? Or was my power taken away from me?

♡ Do I need to forgive myself or anyone else (perhaps your partner, doctor or the hospital system) for what happened in the birth?

♡ Do I wish it were different?

Once you have answered these questions, and spent some time thinking and reflecting on your feelings surrounding the birth, you can start the healing process.

Here's an idea for a meditation that is a really powerful way to rethink your birth. By working through it in your own way, you will not only begin to view what happened with more compassion and kindness, but reconnect with yourself in those difficult times.

Make sure you have some time to yourself when you won't be interrupted, and start by creating a sacred space for you to focus on this. Light a candle, or hop in the bath, or create an environment that feels safe. Once you feel able to let go, start listening to your breath and bring yourself into your body and into the moment. When you're ready, take yourself back to the birth of your baby.

Take yourself into that room.

Feel it. See it. Smell it. Remember it. Remember how it felt.

Don't rush through it – fully breathe into each of the memories, and allow your body to be back in that space. You may feel your heart quicken, or your body tense up, but continue to breathe through it. This is your chance to heal – take your time.

See your face in your mind's eye. What does it look like?

When you're ready, go to that woman in your mind and hold her hand.

Look into her eyes and tell her she is doing an amazing job.

Breathe with her. Tell her again. And again. Surround her with love and energy.

See the power and energy of mother earth around her, and all the mothers who have ever given birth before her. She has all of that energy to call on now.

Wrap it around her.

Then, see your baby being born. Relive that.

The welcoming of their little spirit into this world. That first breath.

If fear or judgement comes up, just smile at yourself in your mind's eye again, tell yourself you did the best you could, and send yourself love.

Tell the woman you see how amazing she is again.

Feel your baby on your chest now. Feel their skin on your skin. See their spirit connecting with yours, just like it did when they were inside you.

Now say to yourself: *I did it. I did it. I did it.*

Your child is here, in this world, because of you. Feel that tingling in your body? That is your power. That is your strength. That is yours forever now. No one and nothing can take that from you.

Open your eyes when you are ready.

WHAT ABOUT WHEN SOMEONE TAKES YOUR POWER AWAY?

We all know toxic people – the ones who suck our energy and strength, making us feel like we're right back at square one again. Perhaps it's the women at school drop-off, your mother-in-law or your colleagues. We all have people who undo the work we are doing on ourselves. And when we're set on moving towards a happier and healthier life, we don't need these people taking our power from us.

Is there anything we can do to protect ourselves?

Years ago, at a day-long workshop with bestselling author Gabrielle Bernstein, I learned a technique to protect myself and my energy which I have used ever since. This is how it works: reach your arms out like you're going to give someone a big hug, and then close them over your chest, as if you're closing a cloak around you. Make sure you really *feel* your arms hugging tight across you. As you do all of this, say (out loud or in your mind), 'I will be loving, and I will be kind, but my energy is mine.'

Put your protection cloak on. You can show up, be kind and still be there for others, but you don't have to give your energy away. And you certainly don't have to let their toxic energy seep into yours.

I will be loving, I will be kind, but my energy is mine.

Inspiring Interview:

Nadine Richardson

Nadine Richardson is the director of the Birthing Institute and creator of She Births, both of which advocate a holistic approach to the birthing process and early motherhood. She began working in the birthing arena as a prenatal yoga specialist and doula over fifteen years ago. She now works with hundreds of new mums- and dads-to-be as they move through the experience of becoming a parent. But what Nadine has to share is not just about birth and it's not just for new mamas either. Her insights into how we can be more mindful, how we can believe in ourselves, and how motherhood can really be our greatest teacher are an inspiration.

We really are so much stronger than we realise. I think as women, our strength is not just in our capacity to be resilient and to move ahead and get things done in that yang/masculine way. It's also very much in our surrender and our softness, our letting go, accepting and adapting. That's the yin energy. And they go together – we have both the yin and the yang. There are times when you will ask: is this a time to be strong and to push through? Or is this a time to just let go and open, be soft and surrender?

Whether it's in pregnancy, childbirth or the early postpartum, in that time of new motherhood there's not one woman who doesn't go through a point of big change. I was talking just the other day to a team of obstetricians at the hospital, and I said to them, 'You know, not one woman gets off scot-free.' At some point you're going to get a crossroad, you're going to hit the hardest part – for some of us it will be during labour, for others it might be in pre-labour, it might be in the pushing stages, it might be in pregnancy (surrendering to continual nausea for forty weeks) – it might be falling pregnant! Some women have fantastic births and have nervous breakdowns afterwards. And it's all part of nature's design – it's to actually *evolve* us; to birth us into more radiant women.

What you learn in childbirth can be used throughout life. In labour your inner dialogue becomes highlighted, and it's important to become aware of it. So much can be learned if we take time to pause and reflect in birth and pregnancy. We learn about how strong we are, we learn about how we surrender and how we let go. We learn about whether we let support in or not – and what we are doing to *block* intimacy and support in our lives.

That is what my clients practise during the birth: a big surge comes and it's intense, and you can either clench up, fight it and get overwhelmed, or you can see what you're doing and realise that you have a choice. You can say, 'Okay, I am just going to accept it. Okay, that was a really big one. That was ginormous, and I don't reckon my endorphins have caught up to the strength of that.' Just be a witness to it. Know that it always passes. We can all take that skill into our lives.

When you're letting go of control, it's also got to be about embracing life and bringing yourself more joy. You need to come at it from a place of seeing what life has to offer right now.

People often see spirituality as something quiet and controlled, and long processes like meditation, but life is not like that when you're in a family, and when you have children and a partner and mortgages. It can be a bit messy. So can you be still, and can you be happy? Can you just be with everything as it is – including the disarray? The messy house? My belief that parenthood is actually a rapid pathway to enlightenment comes from that – from the witnessing of the messy bits. In Sanskrit, there is a concept called '*lila*' which means 'divine play' – it's that ability to watch the natural ups and downs of life, the arguments and the disarray, with a sense of lightness.

Giving birth to my son taught me love. That's the biggest thing I've learned from motherhood. It showed me that I am programmed, not just in the Darwinian way – to survive – but that I am simply programmed to love. There was nothing else in my world the moment Leroy was born. The stillness and the silence; the ability to witness my world and my thoughts … all of a sudden I had these extreme feelings of just love and bliss.

Going through early postpartum, I used to keep saying, 'God, this is just the easiest thing in the world. It's so easy, it's nothing, it's nothing. Everything else is really hard.' All the washing and the cooking and keeping the house afloat – that was hard. But if all I have to do is just love – oh my god. That brought it all home.

If everybody loved the way that a mother loves her child, the world would be healed. There'd be no war, there'd just be harmony and adaptability and conservation of the planet and its resources, because you love and are grateful. So, it's a precious thing. We really need to remember how important mothers and love really are.

'Holding your feelings in
is like putting a steadily
increasing amount of air into
a balloon. There's a limit to
how much air the balloon will
hold before it explodes.'

Doreen Virtue

Chapter  6

Focus 3: Trust

- -
- -

Trust is a big one. For almost every single mother I have connected with or coached, this has been a big sticking point. They just don't trust themselves anymore – whether it's the trust that they can stop the 3pm sugar binges, or get through a hectic morning routine without yelling, or initiate sex with their partners again. It's gone – that faith in themselves.

There's a reason I believe that we need to redefine strength before we move on to trust. If we stick to that old masculine concept of strength, then we'll never build up our trust muscles again.

We'll continually put unrealistic expectations on ourselves that we'll inevitably fall short of, and so where's the trust in that? We'll also fail to see just how strong we already are – despite the sugar binges.

This has been the toughest part for me. It's the bit that has, without doubt, been the most painful lesson to learn (even more than letting go of the superwoman mentality that has dogged me my whole life).

Trusting myself – and believing that I am a good person – has meant I've had to accept all the 'bad' parts of me too.

It's about accepting our shadow selves – that dark part that is the opposite of what we long to be. It's the Mean Mama, the nasty voice, or the lazy girl who tells you to just give up. Your ego.

While I don't want to bombard you with psych words (mostly because I don't know many), this is important for us to get our heads around if we are to begin truly liking who we are in all our multicoloured beauty.

We all have a dark side

I used to have a terrible temper. I would smile and do everything

I thought I should do to be a 'good girl' and be liked, but inside I would be bottling up all my real feelings. Until, like a volcano, angry words would spew out of me like burning lava. I would say the most hurtful things and get so angry my body would shake. I hurt many people I loved.

If stories from my early childhood are to be believed, I've always had that anger. I've always had a bitter tongue, ready to lash out when I was wounded. I would go along with whatever I was told to do, even if I hated it inside, until the explosion.

And then, as I grew, I found that this tendency to lash out meant that I was never understood. My words would sound so consistently acidic that even when I tried to say something nice or word my thoughts in a supportive way, somehow it would be misunderstood. (Little wonder that I eventually developed a thyroid disease – a disease of the throat.)

There were times in my life that I would cringe to remember. I hated this part of myself, and was terribly ashamed of it. If the images of those moments did flash through my mind, my heart would burn and I would just push them further down.

And so, believing that I needed to *change*, I would bite my tongue even harder. I would do even more to please people. I would put myself on hold for family and friends even more, and I would let them dictate my happiness. I would drop everything to be the best sister, and I would go out of my way to try to be the best best friend.

Until, not surprisingly, I would burst again.

Just over three years ago, during that tumultuous third pregnancy, everything changed. For the first time in my adult life, there was a huge rift in my family. It was devastating for all of us, and exceptionally painful, but, like the good girl I wanted to be, I did what I thought I needed to do so that everyone had their space, and I quietly grieved what I thought was the irreversible change in our relationships.

But of course my control didn't last. The anger and hurt I felt was so toxic that one night, when my whole family was together, it spewed out of me in the most horrible way. I was shaking so much even my legs were unstable, and all I kept thinking while it was happening was, *I have to get out of here*. It was like something foreign took over me, and all the hurt came roaring out.

I hated what had happened, and my role in it, and felt like I wanted to disown myself. It was a truly dark time. And in all honesty, I could have done what I'd always done and just swallowed my anger again, begged for forgiveness and not actually discussed why I was so hurt in the first place or how we all needed to address what was going on. Until I did something else destructive. Instead, one very lonely and sad Friday night, I clicked on the website of a gorgeous young woman called Tara Bliss, who I had heard speak just a few weeks earlier, and I discovered that she offered coaching programs. Within minutes, I had signed up.

This beautiful soul helped me to start looking at who I really was, including my shadow self.

The parts you don't like the most about yourself are still *part of you*. They are the dark to your light. They are not to be disowned, or hated, or forced to change. They are a part of your whole.

I used to think that the goal was to be happy all of the time. To never yell again. And while that would be great, it is not my goal anymore. My goal is to lovingly accept myself, see what's going on inside me that has caused that disconnect and to reconnect in whatever way I can. It takes self-compassion and forgiveness.

I don't hate myself when I get angry anymore (which, thank goodness, is not too often). I see what is happening *while* it's happening and acknowledge that it's my shadow self. I own it, look at it and say, 'Oh, I know you.' It is a warning sign that I am disconnecting from myself again. It doesn't mean I'm not all those amazing things I tell myself in my mantra. Let me say that again – *it does not mean I'm not all those amazing things I know I am*. It is simply my shadow self. And to live a full and happy life, I have to embrace it.

Not that it's easy. Please don't be under any illusions that I have this right all the time, and that Mean Mama is banished from my life forever. Nope – she's there. And her favourite mantra is, 'I can't do this anymore.'

As negative, arse-kicking, Mean Mama mantras go, it's a good one. All-encompassing, really. It can be used for work exhaustion, cleaning up vomit, arguing with my husband, or hauling my tired body out of bed after another terrible night of broken sleep.

Whatever the problem, it's got it covered. A blanket 'I give up'. Perfection. It is my default thinking whenever I am struggling.

So why is it still there?

Why, after years of meditating and mindfulness, does this voice creep up and slowly start whispering in my ear, until it grows to such a volume that I actually say the words out loud?

I know it's not because I'm weak. I know that it's not because all of the beautiful focuses and reflections I have done over the years aren't working – in fact, it is only because of that work that I can recognise what that voice really is. And I know it's not because it's true. It's not, and I'm aware of that.

It keeps coming back because it's my default. It's my ego. It's my shadow side jumping in at the slightest opportunity, which is usually whenever more than one child is sick, I've had less than six hours of broken sleep or I've got too many things on my multi-tasking to-do list. It keeps coming back because *that's its role in my life*. This negative thought is there because I'm exhausted, not because I actually can't do it anymore.

Sometimes it takes me a long time to acknowledge exactly what my mind is telling me. That might sound odd, but how often are you aware of what you're telling yourself? Do you really know what your inner voice is telling you as you go about your day, juggling a thousand things or settling an unhappy child all night?

So ask yourself about the part of you that swallows up the trust you are trying to cultivate, and start to accept her too. Awareness is the first step to acceptance.

And while we're talking about acceptance, let me introduce you to the wonderful Brené Brown (and if you already know her, let me remind you of her awesomeness).

Brené Brown is an expert on vulnerability. Yep, she's a university-trained researcher on this topic, and no conversation about vulnerability, happiness, shadow selves or acceptance can be done without her.

What I love about Brené is that she takes all these big concepts like shame, vulnerability, imperfection and authenticity, and makes them step-by-step easy to understand. My Brené books are dog-eared and full of side notes and huge asterisks, and she has helped me accept that being my authentic self — with all my shame, imperfect behaviour and flaws — is the way to live a wholehearted life. These words from her book *The Gifts of*

Imperfection always hit home:

'Authenticity is the daily practice of letting go of who we think we're supposed to be and embracing who we are. Choosing authenticity means:

♡ Cultivating the courage to be imperfect, to set boundaries and to allow ourselves to be vulnerable.

♡ Exercising the compassion that comes from knowing that we are all made of strength and struggle.

♡ Nurturing the connection and sense of belonging that can only happen when we believe that we are enough.

Authenticity demands wholehearted living and loving – even when it's hard, even when we're wrestling with the shame and fear of not being good enough, and *especially* when the joy is so intense that we're afraid to let ourselves feel it.'

We have to learn how to be vulnerable. We have to trust in our own voice and our own intuition, and speak up when we need to. We have to learn how to be the gentle, compassionate mother and the strong, fierce warrior we all have inside us – and the only way to do that is to start cultivating a deep trust in ourselves.

I trust myself now. That's a big thing to say, but I do. I not only trust that I can get through a really tough night with a full day ahead, but I also trust that I can be the compassionate, gentle, loving woman I need to be. Both to myself and to my family. I trust that while I might not always get it right with my kids, I am doing the best I can, and I will know how to pull back, breathe and reconnect when I need to.

Trust Techniques:

 RETHINK YOUR 'SHAME' MOMENT

Learning to trust ourselves is not only about believing in all of ourselves again, but also trusting that there is a lesson in everything. Yes, that old bumper sticker saying 'I have no regrets: everything happens for a reason' sounds lame to me too, but it's true. I may have regrets for the hurt I caused, but there is no way I would be where I am without those moments of shame. As Brené says: 'Owning our story can be hard, but not nearly as difficult as spending our lives running from it.'

So, you know that incident that immediately came into your head when I started talking about my own shame moments? The one that you're still carrying with you? It's time to look at what you learned from it, and how it's helped you grow. It's time to forgive yourself and see yourself in a new light.

What did you learn? How is that pattern turning up in your life still – with your children? How can you turn it into one of life's greatest lessons and start to trust yourself again?

WHAT DO YOU KNOW FOR SURE?

Here's another pearl of wisdom from Ms Winfrey which I've found really helpful in accepting myself and all my imperfections, and trusting who I am. Ask yourself: what do you know for sure?

When I first asked myself this, I didn't really know where to begin. What *did* I know for sure? Not much, it seemed! And without much certainty, there can be no trust. But here's what I did over time – I started to collect little notes of what I knew for sure in my journal.

I know for sure that I can get through a day on less than five hours' sleep.

I know for sure that when I just let go of my perfectionism, everything starts to flow again.

I know for sure that I am loved.

I know for sure that I am the best mother for my children.

I know for sure that the universe rewards the brave.

And I know for sure that when I take time for myself, I am a kinder, more loving, more accepting and more fun woman.

We have to have certainty in this very uncertain world of motherhood. When every day is filled with unpredictability, it's reassuring to know that we can lean on something concrete – something like the trust we have in ourselves and the universe.

Find out what you know for sure, and build your trust again.

Inspiring Interview:

Antonia Kidman

Antonia Kidman is a journalist, media presenter, author, and mama of six! So when it comes to insights into early motherhood, she's got the tips. When I first connected to Antonia, we immediately clicked on the Happy Mama message – she is passionate about supporting women through the massive changes they undergo when becoming mothers, including the importance of keeping their own interests and goals alive.

From the moment a pregnancy is discovered, life changes. The miracle of conception stimulates emotions like hope, happiness, excitement and expectation, but fear and anxiety can creep in too. New motherhood means goodbye to financial independence, spontaneity and the buzz of workplace interaction, and often means a woman feels more dependent on her partner. While new motherhood is a time of great wonder and celebration, it can also be a time of really learning to let go, surrender and trust the process.

I think now, more than ever, new mums are bombarded with information about parenthood – and it's often written information, so it's not tailored to each individual's situation or needs. We've lost that village approach to raising children, so often mothers – just because of the needs of their baby – are home on their own, which can be really isolating. And if you're used to structure, routine and order, then a baby can be really uncomfortable in that sense: it doesn't provide any of that! At least for the first six months; it's a real change in the way you have to operate. I have to admit, that never really sat well with me. I love routine, and I thrive on knowing what I'm doing when, but babies really move against that. It really is, in those early months and years, about surrendering, and remembering that it does settle down. You will get yourself back.

It's also about managing your expectations and your partner's expectations during this time.

I recently read something about the Premier of New South Wales and his comments about his wife's postnatal depression, and he said his reaction was just to withdraw and go in to work. And I think that can be a typical male response, because they don't know what you're going through. Whereas, other females do – the ones that you trust and can be honest with. I could always be like that with my mum, which was wonderful.

It's also a big change to our roles as women. Suddenly, you find yourself in that traditional role of housewife, which can feel really different. Even physically, if you're breastfeeding and you're recovering from a birth, you're different too. Your boobs are doing different things, and you're the only source of food for that baby, which is a huge thing to take on. Personally, I always liked that six-month mark when I could introduce some solids and start to share that responsibility. You do get a little glimpse into this when you're pregnant, because you do share your body, but afterwards it's a real change. While I love the connection that comes from feeding and I think it's a real honour to be able to do that, it's a huge change in your role in life, and you really do have to trust it and go with the flow.

Even if you have the most evolved and enlightened partner, it's still tricky. There's a feeling that you have to rely on them for an income now – for everything, really – and that involves a sense of trust and working out the realities of each other's new roles. And I think the key here is you've got to keep your hands in other pies: you've got to keep your own friends and interests. For your own sense of self, I think it's so important – I've always insisted on this. Even if that means a little bit of work later on when you can, there has to be something that is yours.

That's how I've not completely lost myself with my six children: I've always had a little bit of work. I've always had my own interest that I could pursue. I honestly don't feel like I've ever lost myself over the years – perhaps also because I had such a strong mother. Even now, since we moved to Singapore and my media work slowed down, I have my study [a degree in international law]. Of course my family is so important, but I need something just for me. As a human, I need to have something that I am driven to achieve, and the children fold in around that. They are not secondary to it, but they are part of it. And it's always been like that. I've always had three days where I either work or study, and then the others are with the children – and I'd never give that up! I'm so passionate about it. It's the thing that has sustained me.

Whatever your thing is, even if it's to become really active in the school community, you have to have something. I get the same feeling out of sport – I like to push myself, and not for any other reason than to challenge myself. I now do half marathons and I'd never really done anything like that before my forties, and it's quite extraordinary the mindset you need to be in to be able to get through something like that. But it's the focus on something that is your goal, and no one else's, that is so important when you are raising a family. It's the mental health benefits of exercise that I get so much out of. Of course I need to be strong too to look after the whole lot of them! But a big part of it is that it also turns my mode around. If I don't get to do it, I'm not great, and I don't want to be angry or depressed or down. That plays out on everyone in the family, so I don't look at it as an indulgence. It's actually really important for everyone.

It's good for your family to see you do these things too. It's good to see that Mum's doing a half marathon – and they have to respect what comes with that. They also realise that they can't take all of you – even though they might try!

And the thing is, if you want to prioritise yourself and your own goals, you have to be organised.

I wasn't a naturally organised person, but I think you can train yourself to do anything, and just getting on top of this can make such a difference. I have put systems in place that allow our family to run smoothly. It may take a little while to make it all work, but it pays dividends. It's an investment in the whole family, and if you can prioritise even just a few things for yourself in there, then everyone benefits. Because in the end, if you're okay, then the flow goes down to those around you. It's looking after your family by looking after yourself.

'To love yourself, truly love yourself, is to finally discover the essence of personal courage, self-respect, integrity, and self-esteem. These are the qualities of grace that come directly from a soul with stamina.'

Caroline Myss

Chapter  7

Focus 4: Grace

In the past, when I thought about the word 'grace', my mind was filled with images of Audrey Hepburn and Jackie Onassis.

Women who embodied a certain strength and calm, but also beauty. There was something about this 'grace' that appealed to me, but in all honesty, it felt unachievable. I knew that no good could come of putting people on pedestals and that thinking Audrey Hepburn was always grace-filled is as dangerous as believing the endless picture-perfect images on Instagram. Not true and not useful.

And then I read Marianne Williamson's *Everyday Grace* and I thought, *That's it!* This wasn't just the glamorous, intimidating 'grace' of beautiful women – it was something much deeper. Grace is all about how we act in our daily lives, how we present ourselves to the world and how we respect ourselves. Grace is how we handle a meltdown in the middle of the supermarket, how we put mascara on to brighten our bloodshot and tired eyes, and how we choose to nourish our bodies.

Grace is how we show up in this life, every single day.

And when the shit hits the fan, it's about surrendering to it and accepting that it is what it is.

I'm certain that at times Audrey Hepburn would have cried so hard that she had snot running down her face. Just as I'm certain that in times of crisis (and she certainly had a few!), Jackie O screamed and lost her cool. I am also certain that both women would have had days where they didn't look perfect and simply could not be bothered with anything at all; days where they just lay on the couch in surrender.

And there it is: surrender. How many of us modern-day mamas ignore that key element to happiness. We hang on to our goals and our plans and our set-in-concrete ideals of what our life is meant to look like, and god help us when it doesn't live up to that image. Perhaps this clinging to our ideals is a big part of our disconnection? I know that letting go of all my previous ideas of what a happy life looks like has been a big element in my own healing. Yes, I know the phrase 'just let it go' is chronically overused. ('I just need to let it go? It's so simple, thank you so much for reminding me,' she says, while internally screaming, *I can't just let it go!*) So this isn't any old letting go. This is about opening up to other possibilities.

I once heard a very wise woman describe the way we go through life with our hands clenched tightly around what we want – so tightly it aches. It's like we're hanging on for dear life. But when we understand surrender, and 'let it all go', our hands release, our palms open up, our fingers uncurl from their death-grip and we are open to whatever comes. I loved that. Whenever I think about that analogy, my hands physically soften: I start to let go.

Elizabeth Gilbert sums it up perfectly. We accept what is and 'move on swiftly, with humility and grace. Don't fall into a funk about the one that got away. Don't beat yourself up. Don't rage at the gods above. All that is nothing but distraction, and the last thing you need is more distraction.'

Have faith

Grace is faith. If you want to get technical, we could be talking about faith in a god/goddess/karma/general universal power. Whatever your flavour is, it really doesn't matter, it's about knowing that what happens is not only up to *you*, and that you don't need to have control over everything. The more I go into the spiritual awakening of women as mothers, the more I truly feel that it is our death-grip on perfectionism, control, being on top of everything and having it turn out like we envisioned that is at the centre of our unhappiness. *It wasn't meant to be like this.*

I, like many women, had an image in my mind of a sweet, serene baby, and long catch-ups on perfectly clean picnic rugs in the park with my equally serene mother's group. That's what I equated grace with: an unattainable perfect image. But grace is really about keeping the faith – faith that this is exactly where we are meant to be and exactly what we are meant to be learning. Faith that 'this too shall pass'.

Is there a more powerful mantra for a stressed-out new mama? And after three babies, I know this for sure: everything does pass. I'll get through whatever it is, because I always do. As will you.

As Anne Lamott says, 'Faith includes noticing the mess, the emptiness and discomfort, and letting it be there until some light returns.'

So how do we do that when we really, really don't want what's happening right now? How do we keep the faith and surrender when it's all crap?

We have to work on it, every single day. In my darkest times, when my heart was broken and I doubted any good would come of all that work, I had to physically act every day to connect to my belief that it was going to be okay. I had to get out of my head and that constant replaying of what went wrong – stop myself from fretting over the future, and just get into what I knew for sure. And often, what I knew for sure looked like this:

'I know I can survive this, because I survived [insert crazy time in my past which I'm now amazed I got through]. I now let go of control of this and get out of the way. I drop my planning, worrying and stressing. I surrender to what is.'

As Caroline Myss explains: 'Grace comes in many expressions. It intervenes in raging arguments, calming your anger so that you do not say what you can never take back. Grace whispers thoughts of hope in desperate times, giving you the stamina to hold on through the storms of life. And grace delivers inspiration, awakening creative resources deep within your being.'

We have to surrender and trust that we'll be okay no matter what. We have to stand proud in the face of the screw-up or the tantrum, and know that 'we've got this'. We have to pause during the argument, be mindful of what we are doing, and breathe through it.

The multi-tasking trap

The need for control is rooted in fear – but if we have started to explore the previous focuses of kindness, strength and trust, then we should now be able to recognise that fear as just old Mean Mama patterns that we need to recognise and step away from.

Here's a breakthrough thought that blew my mind when I first recognised it: a truth that would change my life. Multi-tasking doesn't work. In fact, multi-tasking is the source of most of my meltdowns, most of my tears, and most of my shameful mummy moments.

Whenever I have snapped at the kids for asking me the same question over and over again, I've usually been thinking about seven different things. The times I have burst into tears, or thought, *I just can't do this anymore,* or reached for a wine while cooking dinner have usually happened because I've been trying to send an email on my phone while chopping onions and breaking up a sibling fight over who gets to use the pink pen first.

I haven't been present, I haven't been focused on the task at hand and I haven't been in touch with my thoughts. At all. And so what happens? I lose it.

Multi-tasking does not work, mamas. That cliché we were all told as young girls about women being brilliant multi-taskers has backlashed and caused us all to think that juggling a business with babies and a bolognese on the stove is next to godliness – and it ain't. It's the cause of our stress, and at the heart of our dislike of who we are as women and as mothers.

Grace and mindfulness

In the end, I think that's what I loved so much about the idea of Audrey and Jackie. In my fantasy world, they would never have forgotten to buy nappies, they'd never have scrolled through Facebook while trying to fold washing and monitor Play-Doh construction, and they would never have burst into tears because they just couldn't do it all. Yes, this fantasy was unrealistic, but I loved the way they seemed so calm and present – so *mindful*. That's what grace means to me now, being mindful. It's as simple as being aware of your thoughts and doing one thing at a time.

I wanted to be like that. So often I found myself reaching for my phone while breastfeeding my baby. Here was one of the most sacred opportunities for me to connect with myself and my child, and I would be mindlessly scrolling through my feed. My baby would be sucking, with a hand wrapped around my breast, and I would be somewhere else. Other times, I would read my girls a bedtime story and get to the end unable to remember a single word I'd said. It's incredible: we are able to read a story out loud, with animated voices and all, while in our heads we're going over the fight we had with our partners that morning.

I had to learn to give the moment my full attention: see my kids' smiles as they built their Play-Doh worlds, or notice my husband's facial expression as he talked to me about his day. Our children present a million opportunities a day for us to surrender and just 'be', but we are so trained to multi-task that the idea of slowing the mind down and noticing their little breaths or their inquisitive faces is totally foreign.

A child psychologist once told me in an interview that children often share their most intimate thoughts right before bed. There was something about being tucked up, ready for sleep, that opened them up to sharing what *really* happened at school that day – and this has happened so many times with my girls. Right before lights out, one of them will suddenly ask me what happens when you die, or admit that they are being bullied at school. Of course my first reaction is usually, *Really? Right now? But it's already half an hour past your bedtime, the kitchen is a mess, and I've got seven emails to send tonight!* But ever since I've started to try to slow down and be open to more grace, I've breathed past those initial reactions, and centred back in on their little faces.

I don't want to miss this. I don't want to rush through their sharing with me because of what the clock says. I don't want to miss that little hand on my breast as I feed my baby to sleep. Whatever it is – I want to be fully present for it. I want to be out of my head, and *here*.

Grace Techniques:

 KEEPING YOUR COOL

It's all well and good to talk about exuding grace in times of crisis, but how the hell do we do that when the three-year-old has refused to put on her shoes for the past twenty minutes, screaming to the point where you're worried the neighbours will call Child Services, and now you're late for your dentist appointment? Good question. One I've asked myself a lot too.

Here's the very best way I've found to get out of my head and either stop the Screaming Banshee Mama, or at least pull her back as quickly as possible.

Breathe.

Yep, I know, obvious, right? But really, the *second* you notice you're losing your cool, breathe in so your lungs feel like they've just stretched a millimetre further than they ever have before. Find a place deep down in your lungs where the anger and frustration is, and then breathe it out. Feel your shoulders drop, and then do it again.

Feel the cold air coming in through the edges of your nostrils, and all the way into your lungs, and then let it out. We all shallow breathe when we are stressed, so this instantly calms the freak-out hormones and reconnects us with our bodies.

Then, imagine all the angry thoughts inside your head – phrases such as 'I can't do this today!', 'Why does this always happen to me?' and 'Oh, FFS!' Use your breath again, and imagine them moving down through your throat, torso, legs and into the ground.

And then focus on your feet. Ground yourself back into the earth, and into the moment. Only focus on *right now*. What needs to be done first? Do you need to find the shoes? Do you need to give her a hug? Do you need to just keep breathing? Reconnect to the moment.

The more we practise this, the earlier we notice the rising anger or toxic words, and we can pull back.

I once heard Eckhart Tolle speak at an event in Sydney, and he asked us all to start the day by focusing on our hands. Feel our hands, feel the energy of our hands. He was trying to show us how we can use the physical body to ground ourselves. When we are solely focused on a part of our body, we are no longer in the future or the past. We are in the moment.

It works for Eckhart, and it works for me with my kids.

CONNECTING WITH
SOMETHING BIGGER

In the middle of the night, when I'm rocking and shushing and patting the baby for the third hour, grace often escapes me. While I might still be outwardly calm for my baby's sake, internally I am in a world of angst. I'm planning how I'm going to retrain my child so he finally sleeps, I'm running the next day's activities over in my head or I'm just repeating a really mean thing to myself.

In those moments, my greatest strength has come from a connection to what I call 'mother energy' – my way to describe the collective energy of all the mamas who are awake, doing exactly the same thing as me, at exactly the same time. I start by imagining my street, and another exhausted mama struggling to calm her baby. Then the next few streets. And then my suburb. It's like a bird's-eye view over my area, hovering above and seeing into homes where women are trying to be the best mothers they can be. Then, I hover higher, to my city, my state, my country. In my mind's eye I can see thousands of women bound together in mothering, all shushing and patting and trying their best. All in this together.

I breathe in that energy and strength of all these women, and I am stronger again. I feel proud to be part of this tribe, and I know I can get through it.

Inspiring Interview:

Therese Kerr

Therese Kerr was, for much of her adult life, mostly known as the mother of two beautiful children – Miranda and Matthew Kerr. Now she is recognised in her own right as someone dedicated to health and to inspiring others to wellness. Therese is a keynote public speaker, an author and co-founder of The Divine Company (www.thedivinecompany.com), which is committed to creating the purest certified organic beauty products. In my own journey to becoming a Happy Mama, Therese has been a light of wisdom and clarity. I connected with her very early on in my blogging days, and we clicked like old soulmates. We shared a passion for inspiring women to put themselves first, and Therese's insights into her early life as a mother and the importance of balance and self-care have guided me in many ways. To me, she epitomises grace.

I became a mum at a very young age – only eighteen when I had Miranda. I had two beautiful children by the time I was twenty-one, and I devoted my life entirely to them. That's what mums do. And a lot of the time during that period, I really didn't take care of myself.

I lost my own mum when I was pregnant with Miranda. It was such a shock, and I know in my heart it contributed to Miranda being born six weeks early. I can honestly tell you, there wasn't a day went past that I didn't tell my mum I loved her, but I guess it's not until you lose your mum that you truly realise how important she is. We take our loved ones so much for granted. As a young woman with my own little family, I didn't have the opportunity to access her wisdom, and that was heartbreaking. Even now, to not have her here – to give a cuddle to or have a cup of tea with – is such a loss. Things are what they are, though, and we wouldn't be who we are but for our experiences.

I've achieved great success in business and won countless business awards, but the biggest role that I have ever had to play is being a mum. I worked from the time my son was one and Miranda was only three and a half – my husband, Johnny, and I were so young, and we weren't in a financial position for me not to work. If I could go back I would do things differently, but we can't beat ourselves up about our choices. We simply do what we have to with the knowledge we have at the time. Through my working and through the sacrifices we made as a family, my children got to go to private schools. They had their needs well and truly met, they were provided for beautifully and the time we did have together as a family was magical. Many mums now find themselves in this situation – they have to work, and it is important not to beat yourself up over that. I know as a mum I was always torn, and it used to break my heart to drop my children off to the babysitter. You simply make the time you have with your children the most precious it can be!

One thing that I really want to share is that we mums too need nurturing, and we too need to receive. We give so much, and when we give, give, give and we don't allow ourselves to receive, we deplete ourselves. It's so important that we actually learn to self-love, to self-care and to take time out without feeling guilty. I never did that. If there was one thing that I could change it would definitely be that.

A mum's role is so important, and you never stop being a mum no matter what age your children are. You have the role of bringing forth children and raising them to be the most incredible human beings they can be. This includes their physical, emotional, mental and spiritual wellbeing.

It is important to understand that our children learn from everything we do, and they copy us and our actions – most kids want to be just like their mummy or daddy. They pick up on everything: the good, the bad and the ugly. They pick up on the energy within the home, and if you're feeling sad or down, your children will notice. So if you want to take time out to have a cup of tea or go out for dinner with a girlfriend, it is so important that you actually do that. Our social life doesn't finish when we have a baby, we are basically 24/7 carers for our children, and it is okay to ask for time out when needed (minus the guilt, ladies). By doing that, we are also passing acceptance of self-care and self-love on to our children. We are showing them how to nurture themselves.

There's one thing I was never really able to allow myself to feel until probably the past five years, and that is vulnerable. But I now see that vulnerability is a strength, not a weakness. I always saw it as a weakness. I have this attitude of 'I can do anything', and believe me I can – if someone asked me to build a bridge I'd build it. I'll find someone who will do it or who will teach me to do it. But to be able to say, 'You know what, I am not coping right now. I really need a hand', and to reach out to somebody and actually feel good about that as opposed to feeling that I have failed has been so important.

In 2001, they found tumours in my spleen, and in 2002 I had my spleen removed. That was really the turning point for me. I started questioning what on earth I had done to my body.

I thought I was relatively healthy – what caused my body to have endometriosis and then have tumours in my spleen? That's when I started doing holistic healing, metaphysical healing and looking at, 'Okay, what am I actually putting in my body and what am I putting on my body that is impacting on my health in this way?'

I assumed the products on the shelves were safe but was shocked to learn that chemicals are used in everyday cosmetic products on the basis that they are safe until proven otherwise. There's no premarket or health testing done on any cosmetic product before its release, so my business partners and I decided to do something to change this for the current generation and the next by creating healthy certified organic products through The Divine Company.

Since then, meditation has been one of the most amazing practices I have brought into my life. Every morning, I meditate as the sun rises. I sit there and just feel so grateful for everything. I always say to myself, 'How does it get better than this? What else is possible?' When you ask that question of the universe, the universe provides and will show you what else is possible.

I know sometimes it's hard with babies to actually find the time to meditate. I recommend meditating while you're doing the washing or cooking, or while your beautiful baby is asleep. When you're anxious, one of the best ways to switch out of that fight or flight mode is to just really concentrate on deep belly breathing right down into your lower abdomen and all the way up to your shoulders, and then breathe out just through your nose. This will shift you from your sympathetic nervous system state (fight or flight mode) to your parasympathetic nervous system state (rest and repair mode) so your body feels safe enough to burn fat, digest and give you the energy you need to keep going.

If you can allocate yourself twenty minutes that will work wonders. Research shows that twenty minutes of meditation is worth about three hours' sleep! Always try and sit when you meditate and open your heart space. Allow the energy of the universe to filter through you, see it coming and going through your body so you're drawing the universe in and then you're sprinkling it out as well. It creates calm so that you're able to dance with the chaos that life presents without getting flustered.

We are the perfect mums for our children. And just standing in the space of acknowledging that and accepting that this is the most magical experience will bring such peace and acceptance into our lives.

'Happiness cannot be travelled to, owned, earned, worn or consumed. Happiness is the spiritual experience of living every minute with love, grace, and gratitude.'

Denis Waitley

Chapter  8

Focus 5: Value

My mum used to say to my sister and me that the greatest thing she'd ever done in her life was have us – and that used to shock me. *Be a mum? That's it? But what about travel, your career, great moments with friends, Dad!?* Now, with three of my own, I feel exactly the same as my mum used to. This is the best thing I will ever do.

There will be others who will make a greater contribution to the world than me. Other writers will reach more readers; other businesswomen will have more success. There will be other friends who will be there for my friends, and my husband will have other joys in his life than just me. But there will only ever be one mother to my children. They may explore the world and live thousands of miles away from me, but I will always be 'home' to them. Me. Just me. They will walk into my home, or hear my voice on the phone, and I will be able to comfort them and inspire them like no other. That is the greatest role in the world.

But we don't always value that. We were told – either unconsciously or straight to our faces – that being 'just a mum' was a waste of our talent and skills. *What else are you going to do in this world? You can be anything you want!* That was the catch-cry of our generation – and while we can celebrate that it has taken women into roles and positions that our grandmothers would never have dreamed of, it has also completely disconnected us from the very important work of being a mother.

There is an assumption that once we fall pregnant, all we want to talk about is nipples and nappy rash.

It's assumed that we are no longer able to participate in anything broader once we're 'with child'. But while that is a big part of our lives at the moment, we do want to talk about our worth as a woman now that we're not earning as much as we used to – as well as how to juggle the sleep times of two children under two.

The old plan

I was going to be a foreign correspondent. After living in Japan for two years, including a year studying international politics at university in Tokyo, my path was set. Straight after my honours degree I signed up to the ABC as a morning show producer and worked my way up from the backwaters of regional South Australia all the way to Sydney. With it came a whole lot of prestige. Sure, it wasn't Tokyo yet, but I was on my way. I had a plan. Did that plan involve three little ones running around me? Hell, no. I was pretty certain my day-to-day life would look more like *The Newsroom* than *Packed to the Rafters*.

So often the dream we have in our twenties does not live up to our expectations. Influenced by images of Heather Locklear in shoulder pads and power suits, and four single and fantastic gals in New York City, I pictured a life filled with cocktails, promotions and power games. Happiness and satisfaction would come from being more – more skinny, more rich, more successful. The women of my generation were going to rule the world!

But then there was the whole ticking biological clock thing. After years of putting our eggs on hold, we've heeded the warning not to leave it too late, and we're having babies in droves. Often – and certainly in my case – with the secret hope that we can still be that sassy, sexy, successful woman we pictured all those years ago.

That was how I had always viewed motherhood: it wasn't that I didn't want to be a mama: it was in the plans, I guess. At some point. Between the Walkley Award for journalism and the bestselling book which would pay for the New York apartment.

By now we all know how that turned out.

So here's the thing – we can't sit around waiting for society to start valuing our roles as mothers more.

We can't wait for our workplace to start honouring mothers, our government to change its view on stay-at-home mums, or our judgemental neighbours to evolve past their bigoted view of our place in the world. We have to start with ourselves – and each other. Because until we start valuing ourselves as women, mothers, wives and partners, we will always be feeling torn. We will always be reaching for 'more' validation because we don't have it inside ourselves. Like I've said so many times before now, unless we do it for ourselves, we will never find it.

How? I believe we do that in two ways. We redefine success to include our motherhood, rethinking what success actually looks like, and we start to take action in our everyday lives to value who we are and what we are doing.

First, to success.

Redefining success

There's something about the dreams we build as teenagers that are very powerful. Full of hope and hormones, we construct an image of who we are going to be when we grow up, and we make her into a goddess. She is everything we long to become, whether we can see clearly what she does and how she does it, or whether it's just a general 'feeling'.

The thing is, that teenager didn't have a clue what she was talking about. She didn't know about mortgages or mamahood, about endless emails or empty ambition. If she thought that high heels, a cool boyfriend and an exciting job were where it's at, then that's the woman she'd imagine. We all had our own version of that woman, and we've been hanging on to her ever since.

Even after all the work I've done on calming my superwoman ego, I still struggle with this at times. There's a part of me that still wonders if I sold out, or let go of my dream too quickly. I feel like I let myself down because I didn't do what I thought I would, and I'm not where I thought I would be. I've put part of my dreams on hold, even though I thought I never would.

But my family need me. Being a mama and wife is my job right now – and it's taken me a while to be okay with saying that out loud.

This has been big. It's brought up a truckload of issues surrounding women's right to work, my own (outdated) beliefs about success and my own life, what's politically correct, a woman's value as 'just a mum' and judgement. A whole lot of judgement. Why *can't* I have it all? What about my own dreams? And maybe, if I juggle enough, move things around enough, book in some more day care and hire an after-school nanny, I can still get it all …

But when I slow down and look at it for what it really is, I realise: my dreams have changed. My idea of success has transformed, along with my true self, and it's time to let go of that old ideal of what I wanted my life to look like. I don't want to be the stressed out, juggling woman I used to be, and that I used to idolise. I want to be free.

So what does this mean for that woman I've been idolising for thirty years?

It's time to let her go.

It's time to say goodbye (and thank you) to the woman in my mind's eye who is running all the time. She is running to yoga before dawn, running to drop her kids off, running to a hugely successful job where she's admired and rewarded, running to the nanny, running to a date night with her husband. She's got a full calendar, and she's important.

Goodbye, superwoman. You have been with me since I was a little girl and I believed that you were a goddess. I have had images of you on the pin board above my desk for decades, and have judged every decision I made on whether you would do it too. I love you, because you have played a very important part in my life until now, but I don't want to be you anymore. I have changed, and while it's still terrifying at times to not have you there as my goal, I am ready to let you go.

I know a new woman now. She's the one I am becoming. And I'm really okay with that. I'm not going to just say yes to things out of fear of not doing enough anymore.

When we feel undervalued, we tend to start over-compensating by doing *more*. We go above and beyond to prove that we are important, that what we do does matter, that *we* matter. We say 'yes' to more than we should and load ourselves up with extra tasks because we feel like we need to prove ourselves – again.

Saying yes to everything and being everything to everyone is actually undervaluing how important we are. It's so common, especially in women. We take on extra work at our part-time jobs because we're worried that we're not taken seriously. We take on extra roles at school, day care or kindy because we feel like we should be doing more. We even just take on extra roles within our family because we believe we need to: I remember agreeing to look after a great friend's daughter for an afternoon not long after Cass was born because I was 'just at home'. Sure, I *was* just at home – with three kids, including a newborn, and no help. But I wasn't really 'doing anything' …

Can you see a pattern?

It's time to rethink that vision you used to aim for when you were a teenager. Visualise or write down what your ideal day would look like this time next year. Imagine every minor detail.

♡ How do you wake up in the morning?

♡ How do you feel when you first open your eyes?

♡ What do you eat for breakfast?

♡ How are your children and family when you first see them in the morning?

♡ What are their plans for the day?

♡ When do you exercise?

♡ How do you incorporate self-care into your days?

♡ Are there more children? Are you working from home?

♡ How do you feel about your life?

♡ What lights you up?

♡ What does success look like?

Attracting the positive

If you've ever wanted to change your life, find a great relationship or new career, or watched *Oprah*, chances are you would have heard of the 'law of attraction' or 'The Secret' – often discussed as a way to achieve whatever you want in life. At its simplest, it's the idea that like attracts like – if you send out positive vibes, then positive things will come back to you.

It sounds simplistic though, doesn't it? If I just think good thoughts, I'll get that kick-arse job or a mortgage-free life or hot husband … but I actually don't think it's about that at all.

There's a famous story about Jim Carrey and the law of attraction. Many years ago, as a broke and unemployed actor, Jim wrote himself a cheque for $10 million and forward-dated it three years. He kept that cheque in his wallet every day as he went to auditions and struggled to get a break, until eventually his career kicked off. When he landed his role in *Dumb and Dumber* – for which he was paid $10 million – it was almost to the day of the date on top of that cheque.

When he first shared that story, people all around the world pulled out their pens and wrote themselves a cheque. They forward-dated it and assumed that they too would get their Hollywood ending. But of course most didn't. Sadly, it's not that simple.

Working with the law of attraction is about paying attention to how we want to *feel*, not just the things we want – so if you focus on feeling good then you'll get more good feelings. It's not about writing yourself a million-dollar cheque, sticking it to the fridge, then turning around to complain about how little money you have again. We have to back up these actions with more actions. We have to feel it and live it on every level if we want it to happen.

As Danielle LaPorte, author of *The Desire Map,* says, we have this whole goal-setting thing around the wrong way – we need to stop setting goals in the hope that when we achieve them we'll start feeling the way we want to feel. We've all been in that situation where we've sat waiting for something to change (getting married, losing the tummy, having the baby sleep through the night) in the false belief that once it happens, we'll feel good. And then we don't.

What LaPorte has helped me and thousands upon thousands of others see is that we need to start the other way around:

First we need to figure out how we want to feel, and then we must ask ourselves how we can start feeling that now.

Getting my head around this was a big part of how much better I dealt with a newborn – and with the months of broken sleep, brain fog and weariness that come with it – the third time around. By the time my little boy arrived, I'd got pretty good at paying attention to what I was focusing on (ten weeks on the couch will do that), so when it came time to get through the first year again, I just didn't think about the sleep thing. I mean it: I didn't count the times he woke, and I didn't discuss his sleep with the mums at school. I even banned my husband from asking me how the previous night was when I came downstairs bleary-eyed.

When we start to find ways to feel the way we want to now – whether we want to feel valued, seen, acknowledged, beautiful, sexy, powerful, loved, celebrated or divine – then there is no more waiting. That good ol' law of attraction just keeps sending us more. And we find ourselves surviving previously tough situations in our life with grace and ease.

And, hand on my heart, honest-to-god, I got through those sleep-deprived months better than I ever did with the first two. Despite the fact that number three was actually the worst sleeper of them all.

Honouring yourself

Before we wrap this whole value thing up, I've got one last point that I think is really important: how you feel about yourself matters. If you don't value who you are, and think, *What's the point anyway, no one is going to see me today,* then guess what, mama? You'll just keep getting that vibe over and over again.

We have to start treating our days with respect and our place in the world with honour if we want to feel respected and honoured. And, in my experience, that includes the way we dress and present ourselves.

This has been a tough topic to discuss. The first time I wrote a blog about putting on something that makes you feel good every day, I received a heartbreaking email from a reader. Why would I make mums feel the pressure to be beautiful on top of everything else they have to do?! There were days when she could only just manage to put her tracksuit pants on, and it was not my place to make her feel bad about that.

I was so devastated by this email that I retreated from this topic for a very long time. But you know what? I stand by that blog now. I've spent a lot of time reflecting on this, and it's clear to me that how we feel about ourselves is reflected in how we present ourselves. If we are to fully love, accept and celebrate ourselves as women again, then for god's sake we need to feel good!

I don't care if it's your tracksuit pants that make you feel divine or if it's your oldest skirt that has a few baby stains on it. Remember, this is about how you *feel*. Before babies, we used to get dressed in a certain way every day to present ourselves to the world as we wanted to be presented. We may have had our work clothes, our social clothes, our 'looks'. It was part of our identity. And yes, a true spiritual yogi does not concern herself with how she looks, but I'll assume you're still on my level of awakening and are not ready to live without some nice things.

So it starts with mascara. Or hand cream, or bright red lipstick, or your favourite earrings. Just one little act can be the catalyst for a whole transformation in how you feel about yourself – and for me that act is putting on mascara. If I focus on it in the morning rather than just mindlessly getting ready and rushing out the door, I've started a connection with myself. This isn't just about hiding tired eyes and wrinkles: it says to the world, *Yes, I'm showing up today*. I'm shattered, and I haven't shaved my legs since last summer, but I'm here. I'm doing my best. And I'm worth the effort.

Value Techniques:

 WARDROBE CLEAN-OUT

I love this technique! Clearing out your wardrobe is meant to be a reflection of your transformation: shedding the old you, the parts that you've been hanging on to 'just in case'. No more putting yourself on hold and waiting for the body/job/baby to change.

If you don't love it, donate it. If it doesn't suit you now (you know that tight, tight skirt that you loved ten years ago?), then pass it on. If you don't feel your best in it, move it on.

In our society we have an obsession with having a big wardrobe – even if it means collecting clothes that aren't right for us. But that just leaves us overwhelmed in the mornings with the sense that we 'have all these clothes and nothing to wear'.

If it's not who you are anymore, let it go. Make room for the best. Clear out the clutter.

And while you're at it, clean out your bathroom cabinet, makeup bag and underwear drawer: old hair products that you never use, clumpy mascara and blue eyeliner. Maternity bras and knickers with the elastic gone. Why do we hang on to this stuff?

Ask yourself: who am I now? What makes me feel confident, happy and proud?

You deserve to feel that every single day.

This is not about buying lots of new things and spending money on material possessions. It's actually about being super clear on what we need in our lives, being mindful when we reach into our bathroom cabinet in the morning and treating our morning routine like the beautiful ritual it should be. We're telling the universe that we only want the best.

SET UP A NEW REWARD SYSTEM

This idea came from my friend and former coach Tara Bliss. In her book *High: A Party Girl's Guide to Peace*, she talks about ways in which former 'party girls' can start to set up new reward systems – other than reaching for that wine or line. And as I read those brilliantly written pages, it occurred to me that this is a very important lesson for mamas too.

How do you reward yourself for all the things you do? What's your daily ritual of celebrating another day as a mama, partner and woman?

And, when it's been a really tough day, how do you acknowledge that you got through it and you did the best you can? Do you mindfully choose something, or just reach for whatever is easiest, and block it all out?

Do you reach for a wine ? Or dive into the chocolate? Or mindlessly switch on the TV or scroll through Facebook? Do you tell yourself you 'deserve' it?

Now, just for a minute, think about what would happen if you started to value yourself, your body, and what you do every day more? What would happen if you saw the end of the day celebrations as a chance to validate your role in your family, and to honour how important you are?

This is not about having that wine if you really want it, or indulging in a little dark chocolate with your fave reality TV show – it's about mindfully and consciously choosing something that fills your need at the time without depleting your body and soul.

Some simple ideas that you can start to do to set up a new reward system are:

♡ light a candle

♡ turn down the lights and put on some music

♡ make a cup of tea or another favourite comforting drink in a special cup and slowly take that first sip

♡ mindfully put on your comfy slippers or ugg boots and feel your whole body relax

♡ spend five minutes stretching into your body

♡ run a bath

♡ choose an aromatherapy oil to fill your house with a lovely scent

♡ tell yourself you rock!

Inspiring Interview:

Julia Jones

Ayurveda is a traditional Indian system of medicine that can show us different ways of looking at health. In particular, it has a beautiful approach to motherhood. After my son's birth, and with my new commitment to focusing on my healing, I stumbled across the work of Ayurvedic postnatal doula and teacher Julia Jones. Her book *Nourishing Newborn Mothers* was my bible in those early days, and since then I have gone on and trained under Julia to understand how to support mothers during the postnatal time. Her insights though, as you'll see below, are not just about post-birth. They are about our journey as mothers – forever.

We live in a very baby-centric culture. We have baby showers and baby naming ceremonies, and all the gifts at these events are for the baby too. Mothers are experiencing probably the biggest transformation they will ever face, with no acknowledgment of their unique physical and emotional needs.

Even the visitors want to know how big the baby is, what's the baby's name, can they hold the baby – and the poor mum's often just left in the background going, 'I have no idea what just happened to me! I am a different person and everyone expects me to be the same and I can't even think straight. I don't know who I am anymore.' It can be a really tumultuous time.

We're so fixated on birth too – which of course is super important – but once it's over, mums go, 'Oh, and there's a baby. I didn't really prepare for this.' Even more shockingly, we realise, 'I know and see and experience the world in different ways now that I'm a mother.' I think we really miss this point in our culture. We build up so much fear and worry around birth, and then completely forget about those first six weeks afterwards.

These first six weeks are considered very important in so many ancient cultures. Dana Raphael is an anthropologist who studied nearly two hundred ancient cultures and found that they all have nourishing traditions for a newborn mother. These include things like food, massage, heat treatments and all sorts of different ways of celebrating and honouring that change. The children are the future, so if you look after the mum then she's in a really strong position to be the mum she wants to be. And that lasts a lifetime.

After I had my first baby I was working as a doula, and I did a breastfeeding course with Christina Smillie, who's the most incredible lactation consultant and paediatrician – she's leading the world's research on breastfeeding. And she really brought to my attention this idea that 'baby brain' isn't a disability, it's not a problem. And it's only considered a bad thing because we live in such a masculine society where logic and rules and math are the only qualities that are considered important and valuable.

But when you consider the way the human species has evolved, if you really think about what is the most important thing for the continuation of our species, it's mums being super-smart. Mums have got to get their brains working right. Newborn mothers are primed to have the really high oxytocin levels – the love and bonding hormone – right at the time that we give birth, and that oxytocin continues for the first few months and even years afterwards. Your whole brain is marinated in that oxytocin, and it changes completely.

When you actually look at scans of brains of women who haven't had children yet and women after having children, it's a totally different brain. It is absolutely a physical transformation. We get a better sense of smell, touch, sight, sound – which all makes sense because we need to be super alert to protect our babies. We also have better empathy and compassion. We're better at reading body language and non-verbal cues. This time of change after giving birth is what my teacher Ysha Oakes referred to as a 'sacred window'. Many traditional medicines and cultures have their own terminology and symbols to express this opportunity for rewiring the brain for love and peace, forever.

I think we just need to stop thinking that there's only one right way of being, that there's only one brain that's useful in society, and accept that this is the mothering stage and this is what my brain needs me to do right now.

Even though I had already trained as a postnatal doula, I didn't have this understanding after my first baby. I didn't understand what was happening in my brain. It really threw me. I was having the right physical nourishment, and I was having the massage, and I had my mum helping out. But I didn't have any kind of framework for understanding that inner transformation and what was actually happening on a biological and hormonal level. I was lost. I really was. It was a terrible, terrible time in my life and I hate to say that looking back.

But it's never too late. I had a very healing experience with my second, and I have also talked to lots of people who have healing experiences much later.

That healing starts with compassion towards ourselves. I always find women are so compassionate towards their babies. They argue, 'He's tired, he's having a bad day', or 'He's grumpy because he's sick.' And yet we don't have that same level of compassion and understanding towards ourselves. We tell ourselves that we are a bad mum, or we feel really guilty, or we say, 'That was a stupid thing to do.' But if we could start talking to ourselves and modelling our self-talk on the way we feel and talk about our children – that alone can start a huge transformation.

You can't sacrifice your own needs and then expect your baby to be happy even if you're not. It's like the rule on an airline – put your own oxygen mask on first. We have to come to learn as mothers that we can't last very long without our own reserves being restored.

There's so much external pressure on mothers, and so little acknowledgement of what inner transformation is going on. Often we cling to other mothers at the same stage as us – it's like a life raft. You just need to find someone who's going through that same feeling as you are because you can't talk to anyone else about it.

Even talking to your own parents, your own mum, friends

without children, friends who had children ten years ago is a great idea. When you're really in that moment there's nothing more comforting than other people saying, 'It's normal, you are not crazy, I am feeling that too.'

Wouldn't it be great if our culture supported mothers the first time around, right from the beginning, and really encouraged self-care for a new mum? It really breaks my heart to hear how many people are suffering – and to hear someone say they still have postnatal depression ten years later. It doesn't have to be that way. Not in the vast numbers that it is. Not if we had a culture of care.

If you feel like you missed your sacred window, then re-do it! I've sometimes encouraged mums to take a 'baby moon' months or even years after those early weeks of motherhood. Take some time out for you and your family to do things that increase your oxytocin and brain plasticity – there are actually many ways you can do this. Spend time cuddling and eating yummy food and having massages and baths and walks on the beach. This stuff is not a luxury, it's how you rewire your brain for peace and joy – forever! It's the best gift you can ever give your children.

'Once you connect with yourself, it is impossible to be lonely or desperate.'

Bryant McGill

Chapter

Focus 6: Connection

In the middle of 2015, I was invited to speak at a life coaching event in New York City. Not in my wildest dreams had I envisaged this one coming my way (which goes to show that when we surrender and just do what we love, we often get more than we ever imagined), and my first reaction was 'Hell yes!' followed quickly by, 'Oh my god, I can't do that.'

I had three kids. I had a husband who works ridiculously long hours, and I had zero savings to pay for this extravagant trip. But, in a total leap of faith well beyond anything I actually believed I was capable of, I said yes and promised I'd find a way.

Six months later, the stars, the bank account, and some babysitter offers all aligned, and I was about to fly to New York. We had miraculously found a way to get all three kids looked after (thanks to brilliant friends and a generous sister), so that my husband and I could go together. It felt over-the-top, scary and slightly irresponsible, but the biggest feeling I had was fear.

Ten days in New York – just the two of us. No children to interrupt, no babies waking in the night. There would be no rushing home for naps or being woken pre-dawn after a rare date night. It was just me and my man alone for more than a week, for the first time in nearly eight years.

What if we didn't get along? What if we didn't have a connection? What if I just didn't feel it anymore?

I would define my marriage in the way that I think most married couples with young children would: pretty good, but in need of some TLC. Whenever we finally did organise a night out on our own, we always had a good time, and our communication was good … as long as the baby had slept, our jobs weren't too busy and we hadn't had three kids' birthday parties in one weekend. But ten days on our own?

Where have 'we' gone?

Babies turn even the most loving partners into mere acquaintances raising children together. Our roles change, our sex lives change and our deepest desires change – often to sleep. When kids come into the picture, we primary carers can go from having the same income, social life and dreams as our partners, to suddenly feeling like we have put our lives on hold for our families. Meanwhile our partners get to just keep on going the way they always have.

As advanced as we have become in many areas of women's rights, the fact remains that a man's career is rarely interrupted by him having children in the way a woman's is. As journalist and author (and mama of three) Annabel Crabb asks in her book *The Wife Drought: Why women need a wife and men need a life*, why do we assume that women will change the way they work after they have kids, but that men's work lives will continue unchanged?

We either put any work outside of the home on hold or struggle through years of guilt at not being fully present at work or with our kids. And even if you are happy to be home raising the kids, there's the judgement that comes with that.

Then in walk our partners, back from their 'normal' lives, to find us knee-deep in domesticity. 'What did you do today?' How I used to hate that question! *What do you think I did today?* I wanted to scream. *Only breastfed every couple of hours, washed everything in sight, went to the shops again – oh, and wait for it, watched* Play School *four times!* No wonder there's not much going on in the bedroom.

Not that we feel like it anyway. Our bodies have changed in such a way that they are often unrecognisable, and we're worried about 'bits' that might not be appealing anymore. Whoever was the first person to make the suggestion that a man won't want to have sex with you after they have witnessed you giving birth owes married parents everywhere a serious apology. And payment for couples therapy.

Here's the thing, though: physical intimacy with your partner and a connection that goes beyond sorting out family schedules is an important part of your life. It's passionate, it's sensual, and it's really integral to our happiness as women. I'm sure at one stage it was a big part of your relationship, and I don't know about you, but I don't want to go the rest of my life without experiencing passion again.

But how do you get it back when it's been months between events? How do you turn it on when you know the baby will be awake again in two hours and you *Just. Want. To. Sleep*? And how do you even feel like it again when all you are doing is talking about the kids' schedules and what's for dinner?

Which brings me back to my New York story. A week before the Big Apple trip, I was talking to my mentor and it all came pouring out. My worries, my concerns, my nervousness. What if it's not okay?

What she said to me literally changed my marriage in an instant: 'You have to stop thinking about him and what he can give you, and start focusing on yourself and what you can give yourself on this trip.'

What she meant was: I was pinning the whole trip on how *he* was going to make me happy, make me feel good, make me feel beautiful, sexy, sensual and alive again. Which, as anyone who has ever put such expectations on a relationship would know, is a recipe for a screaming match on the first night followed by nine days brooding over divorce.

I had to figure out what I longed for and think about how I could give that to myself.

Marianne Williamson describes this problem in terms of primary and secondary relationships. Our primary relationship is with ourselves, because all else flows from there. When we get the primary relationship right, then our marriage, our children, our careers, our family, our community, every other relationship is improved.

So what I needed to do was to work on my primary relationship first. I needed to connect back to me. Which isn't easy when you feel like your sex life has been put on hold.

Rebuilding the connection

A mama I coached once said to me, 'I'm just all cuddled out', and I thought that was such a great explanation of how it can feel at the end of the day. When you've been so physically attached to your children all day – feeding them, cuddling them, picking them up, carrying them around – a hand suggestively reaching out for yours at night can feel like too much. There is no way we can switch it on in bed if we've poured all of our energy and love into a demanding little child (or three). There's nothing left.

Our partnerships must be given the space to be nourished, just as we have to find space to nourish ourselves. We literally have to 'turn it on'. We have to connect with ourselves before we can connect with a partner – whether in the bedroom or just hanging out on the couch. When I heard Marianne speak on this, she explained to a captivated room of women that it takes at least half an hour for us to switch out of our masculine mode of doing, doing, doing, and into our feminine mode of just being. Half an hour. That means half an hour of actively switching your feminine energy on. Having a bath, lighting a candle, listening to music. *Not* doing the dishes and sorting out the day-care bag for tomorrow.

Every relationship (regardless of gender) is a dance of masculine and feminine energy, and for most people if both partners are in one space, then it ain't happening. Nothing you can do about it – it's just not there. It's two yangs (or yins) clashing, and there's no spark (well, not the good ones anyway).

I once attended a tantric workshop interestingly called the 'Soulful Bedroom Goddess Workshop'. (Just as research for this book of course.) In this group of about twelve women, every single one of us struggled with intimacy in some way. One couple had recently had children and didn't know how to get the spark going again. Another had been married for years and things had faded out. Some were young and dating but felt very insecure about sex. It was so interesting to sit and be a part of what felt like an ancient sharing of wisdom about sex, passion and feminine energy, and I sat there wishing that it was a more widely accepted discussion in our culture.

What I learned that night (other than that there are five different types of orgasm!) was that passion and intimacy are all about energy exchange. It's about giving as well as receiving. If we have no energy left to give, we have none to receive.

So before I got on that plane to New York, I needed to build up my own energy. I needed to stop putting all my expectations on my husband to provide what I so desperately wanted, and find a way to give it to myself first. Which meant instead of looking to him to feel connected, to feel special, to feel validated, I needed to do that myself.

And it worked. Over the following ten days, not once did I feel like I had to ask for what I needed or demand anything from him. It flowed, just like it used to before we had children. We had the space to slow down and get to know each other as well as the streets of New York. We could hold hands without other little hands trying to squeeze in the middle.

I had dropped my expectations, and with the space that only time without children can allow, we found each other again.

Parenthood will pass. These crazy-arse days of endless focus on our little ones will be just a small part of our entire lives – and hopefully, our entire relationships. The knowledge that I could find a connection again when the kids were away was one of the best feelings I've had in a long time. But I have to be honest: it's been a struggle to hang on to it now that we're home again. We're back to the realities of nappies and night wakes and school concerts and swimming lessons, and disconnection is a very real threat.

On tough days, I try to remember to take some time after the kids are asleep to 'switch on' first. I wash my face, I dim the lights in the kitchen, I light a candle. I go slow, and I don't reach for my phone. That night, even if I really, really don't feel like it, I remember how important this relationship is to my own happiness too, and I reach my hand out to hold his as we fall asleep.

Friendships

It's not just our partners we long to reconnect with. We miss our sisterhood too. Raising our babies as a group of women – standing with our tribe. We were never meant to have babies in isolation, spending the majority of the day talking to no one but our toddlers.

Friendships can be tough with kids. Unless you're having them at exactly the same time as your girlfriend, you may well be dealing with kids at different ages, which can mean very different lifestyles. Not that having children of similar ages is always the recipe for strong bonds – mothers' groups are either a huge hit or miss for so many mamas. I lucked out with mine, a wonderful group of women that I am still in contact with, despite now living interstate.

But with the birth of my third baby on my own in a big city, I missed that regular contact so much that I created my own little mothers' group. I reached out to two friends who had babies around the same time as me, and set up a fortnightly rotating lunch date: every two weeks, we would meet at one of our homes for lunch, a sneaky glass of bubbles, and a download of the realities of our lives.

It's hard work keeping our friendships alive post-babies. Before bubs, our friends were key to our happiness and a big part of our lives. Girlfriends are meant to be forever, right? Carrie and her gals could manage it, so can we! Babies won't get in the way of our bond (just like they're never going to get in the way of our sex lives).

Suddenly, our friendships have to fit in around everything else. Text messages before bed, rushed phone calls on the way to work, quick catch-ups after months of rescheduling: welcome to the friendships of motherhood. Career, responsibilities, romances, marriage and now babies mean our former number-one priority slowly slips down our list of frequently dialled numbers. And while some rare female friendships readjust to this change in status easily, many don't. Which can be heartbreaking, coming right at a time when we desperately need to feel a connection with another woman.

In researching for a magazine article about female friendship in your thirties, I spoke with Natalie Kon-yu, editor of *Just Between Us: Australian writers tell the truth about female friendship*. She was pretty clear that the expectations we have of our female friendships – thanks partly to the media – can be harmful.

'*Sex and the City* was such a rare space in our cultural landscape,' she told me. 'It allowed us to hear women talking to each other about the realities of life, but the idea that four such different women can continue to get along despite the fact their lives change immeasurably is completely unrealistic. It's a myth, and I think it's actually damaging to women, because you tend to blame yourself if you can't hold on to your friendships like that.'

'I remember when my best friend and I fell apart,' admits Kon-yu. 'I felt so ashamed of myself at not being able to maintain that friendship the way I thought I should.'

It's often no one's fault – it's just part of our transformation. In fact, research has found that we end up replacing about half of our friends every seven years, which means that if you were picking five or six bridesmaids out of the women you feel closest to today, chances are that two or three of them would have been different had you been picking seven years ago. And again two or three of them would be different in another seven years.

Nothing is permanent. Not our lives, not our relationships. The fact that I didn't have my best friend from my teens and twenties at my baby shower, like I was convinced she would be, has been painful, but I see it now as part of my growth and change. The space she left was for new amazing and supportive women to enter.

Connection Techniques:

 A REGULAR DATE WITH YOURSELF

If we want to feel anything other than tired, bitter and rundown, we've got to book in some time alone. Just us. No babies or hubbies or friends or sisters. And it has to be guilt-free. Sure, we can do the spa day, with the facials and massages – that's what everyone thinks of when we think of 'me time', isn't it? But most mamas I know who finally book in the pamper day spend the whole time at the spa feeling guilty that they're there! So I say, if you can't do it without the guilt, then there's no point in doing it.

A regular date with yourself can be a coffee every Tuesday after school drop-off, where you do nothing but read your book. It can be going to a movie once a month. It can be starting those French lessons, going back to yoga, going for a run on the beach every Saturday morning. And if you want to get your partner to really enthusiastically support your alone-time? Tell them that by doing something like this for yourself, you might be more ready to connect in 'other ways' later. That should work.

A FRIENDSHIP DATE
AND A DAY DATE

In my article on friendship, one of the authors I spoke with threw in the suggestion that we should 'date our girlfriends'. I loved it! If we want our friendships to survive the tumultuous years of parenthood, we have to invest in them. We have to do more than just ring when we want to bitch. We have to send supportive texts. We have to randomly call just to see how they are. We have to pick up an extra coffee sometimes and drop it around 'just because'. And we most certainly need to book in a regular date night.

But when it comes to spending time with your partner, I'd suggest taking date nights *off* the table. I've always found that there's too much pressure, and they take too much organising to happen often enough. Breastfeeding, waking overnight, co-sleeping: getting someone else to put your kids to bed and keep them in bed is a big ask for most new parents. (Unless you're blessed with very generous grandparents, and in that case, what are you waiting for?!)

In my world, date days are much, much better. The first time I went out with my husband in daylight without a child attached to me was liberating. I couldn't believe how different it felt. Going out to lunch and not rushing home for naps was like *freedom*. We took our time, wandered around without being pushed over by drunk teenagers or flirty twenty-somethings. We could hear each other in the restaurants, and didn't need to fight for a cab to get home. Plus we were back in time for cuddles with the kids just before popping them into bed and having the night to ourselves anyway! Seriously, day dates are the thing.

Inspiring Interview:

Grace Gedeon

When Marianne Williamson – author of *A Woman's Worth* and creator of The Aphrodite Training – came to Sydney to talk about relationships, I was front and centre. And when she referred to a Sydney counsellor as the woman she talks to about her own relationships, I frantically wrote down the name: Grace Gedeon. So, when it was time to pull together some insights into marriage, partnership and connection, I thought, 'Who else to ask but the woman Marianne asks?' Here are life and relationships coach Grace Gedeon's reflections on our most important connections.

For many people, relationships are about getting a love that they longed for. That's what is at the core of it. And so if they were longing for love from an external source and then they found it in their partner, they feel fulfilled when they're getting it from their partner. Then when they have a child, they have an alternative source to get their external love. So sometimes people just go and transfer the source of love from being the partner to being the child. In other words – they get fulfilled from somewhere else.

Another reason for disconnection I see is the responsibility we feel as a parent. When a parent becomes responsible for a child sometimes they become overwhelmed – it's not that they prefer or enjoy that sort of love more than their partner's, it's just that they give so much to that child that they feel drained.

So really, two of the reasons for disconnection are: people who are looking for an external source to receive love from can swap sources from their partner to their child, and people who are over-responsible give so much away to the child they have nothing left for their partner. Both are about a disconnection from their self.

If you've done a lot of work on yourself before you have children, you can slow down and take time to connect with yourself, connect with your partner and include it all in your new role. But for most new mums, they simply don't have the time or space to do this. They're running around, they're cleaning, they're working, they're worrying, they're trying to get their body back into shape. They've got so much on their plate, they don't have the luxury to connect with themselves, or with their higher power or the universe. They're too busy just trying to connect with their child. And the thing is, connecting takes space and time and effort, whereas the other stuff you can almost do in a trance. You have to consciously connect.

Becoming a mother often means a redefining of your identity. It means defining yourself as 'a mother' – which can sometimes feel like you're losing yourself, because with motherhood comes a great deal of responsibility. Often, the first time you have responsibility for someone else.

When you're a little kid, your parents look after you, so it's all about *you* because you are getting nurtured and raised. And then as you grow older and you grow into your teens, it becomes about your identity as separate from your parents, so there's that rebellious phase. Then, when you go into your twenties, you start developing as a woman and ask, 'Okay, what am I doing with my life?' You tend not to have too much responsibility for anyone else. It's all about, 'Here I am. I am going to go to uni, or I am going to get this job. Or I am going to do this career, or I am going to work out, or I am going to attract this man, or I am going to travel to Europe.' So you make all these choices for yourself. That is where a lot of women feel most empowered, when they're going through that phase where they're making independent choices for their individuality and themselves.

But then they start having children and there's a whole new dynamic. For the first real time in their lives, they're responsible for someone else. And they don't really know how to look after themselves *and* the other person adequately.

That's why they lose themselves. That's where the collapse happens. Because this is a very, very vulnerable being that they have to look after. They have to make sure they don't break them or damage them psychologically, physically, emotionally, mentally, spiritually. It's a big responsibility, and emotionally they start to abandon themselves.

I think the biggest thing when it comes to reconnecting with your partner is the simplest thing, which is asking, 'Can we talk?' The important thing to remember here is that if one person says, 'I don't want to talk about it now', don't push them. We are told, 'Oh, communication is so important', but that's not communication, that's badgering. So instead, say, 'Okay, sweetheart, I understand you don't want to talk about it now. But I am really upset, and I really want to talk about this – can we please make time to talk about this later?' And you need a partner who's willing to say, 'Yes, I will talk to you later.'

Communication is about honouring one another, and using your intuition. I understand it's hard; it's hard to find the balance between the soft, giving feminine, and the masculine energy of asking for what you want. But we have to give our relationship space to thrive. We can't just give everything to our child – we have to nurture our partnerships too.

And finally, working on our self-esteem is vitally important both within our relationships and within our lives in general. And when I say 'self-esteem', I mean it in two ways. The first is in the way we value ourselves as women. It's the belief that we value ourselves just because we exist. Not because of our job, or our role, or our responsibilities – but because we *are*. The self-esteem of being-ness. So to develop that, it's important to go and read works like Marianne's *A Woman's Worth*.

The second way is what Edmund Bourne describes as the way of acting, thinking and feeling that demonstrates how you accept yourself, respect yourself, trust yourself and believe in yourself. So, ask, 'How am I acting? How am I thinking? And how am I feeling? And how are those actions, thoughts and feelings demonstrating self-acceptance, self-respect, self-trust and self-belief?' It's a little bit of a formula, and it works really well. When we build that self-esteem up, our relationships then become stronger.'

'When you surrender to what is and so become fully present, the past ceases to have any power. The realm of Being, which had been obscured by the mind, then opens up.

Suddenly, a great stillness arises within you, an unfathomable sense of peace. And within that peace, there is great joy. And within that joy, there is love. And at the innermost core, there is the sacred, the immeasurable, that which cannot be named.'

Eckhart Tolle

Chapter 10

A Mindful Mama is a Happy Mama

Over the past eight years of motherhood, I have screamed at my kids in complete self-pity too many times to admit. I have slammed doors on their little faces when it was time for bed and all I could think about was getting into bed myself. I have said no to stories, to treats, to movies and to more playtime because I was wrapped up in my own woes and couldn't pull back. And I have cried and cried, hiding in the bathroom, begging for it to be different.

As they say in the classics, it didn't happen overnight, but it did happen. It started with mascara, and affirmation cards, and a desperation to start feeling happy again. It started with the idea that I didn't have to put myself on hold while raising my babies, which then became the realisation that I didn't even want to be that woman I used to idolise anymore. It started on that hospital bed two years ago, with my very first chakra meditation, and a complete surrender to the situation.

Mindfulness is not just for the yoga mat, or the class once a week. It isn't about being a guru or doing everything right.

It's about stopping and connecting with your thoughts – and then choosing to focus on kindness. Strength. Trust. Grace. Connect with yourself. Know that you can do this. Transfer that compassion you feel for your children whenever they struggle to yourself. Mother the mother.

Motherhood is changing

This is an important time in our world, and we are at the centre of it. I know you may not think you are, sitting at home, with ironing and school lunches on your to-do list. But we are. It is well-documented that the way to change the world and combat poverty is to teach women the skills to farm and run small businesses – because they, in turn, pass on those skills to their children and their village.

Well, we are in a spiritual poverty. And the only way out is for us to learn the skills to reconnect to our spirits. This is what that opportunity is: a chance to turn around the connection depletion sweeping the world and show our children – who have the chance to truly change the way things are done – that there are different kinds of success.

The Dalai Lama said during a 2009 Vancouver Peace summit that the world will be 'saved by the Western woman'. You can imagine how this statement ricocheted around the world. Some loved it, others condemned it. But at the very core of it, what I and many others believed he was referring to was the power and opportunity the Western woman has right now to start doing things differently. To change the way we approach success, globalisation, war, poverty. We have a voice, and we're starting to use it. In small doses, sure – but it's there.

The world is changing. While we may not realise it as we struggle to feel valued – doing day-care drop-off or another class of Baby Bounce and Rhyme, there is a tidal wave of awareness beginning to rise around the importance of what we do – of the role we play. But if we are to take that wave and ride it, we have to come together in understanding that we *can* play that role. That what we do is essential.

Motherhood is our greatest teacher.

The shame and guilt I felt after Scarlett's birth was my spiritual labour. It was the pain of my soul cracking open, and the disintegration of every single belief I had about myself. I thought that if I tried hard enough, studied more and asked the right people the right questions, I would be the perfect mother. I thought there was such a thing as a 'perfect mother'. And my darkest hour came when I realised that absolutely none of that was true, and all I could do was surrender.

From that darkness came light. Just as those final centimetres of dilation are the most painful before we are ready to push our baby into the world, so too are our own births as mothers. Just as in labour, the more you fear it, the harder and longer it will be. We are being born. We are giving birth to a woman who is stronger, more empathetic, more spiritual and connected than she's ever been before, and she is magnificent.

Committing to happiness

Yogi Bhajan – the founder of Kundalini yoga – teaches that the very first principal in connecting with happiness is 'commitment'. If we are to be truly happy, we have to make it a priority. It has to be more important than anything else, because as we've seen over and over again now, when we are happy, everyone around us is too.

We can't just wait around for that happiness. I can promise you that waiting for the baby to sleep, or school to start, or your husband to initiate sex again is not the answer you are looking for. The answer is a promise to yourself that you are going to show up every single day and be present. You are going to *see* your children and how they are growing. You are going to honour your body and how it has changed. You are going to slow your mind, stop the judgement, and start to connect to something again. You are going to find a way.

It may not happen every day. In fact, let's be clear here and say it won't. But that is not an excuse for us to give up. We are worth more than that.

Show up. Make a commitment. Put your happiness first.

This is not about the amount of time you spend with your children. A Happy Mama can be a woman who is working full-time or is a home-schooling always-on mum. The important thing here is how you are reconnecting to your spirit, not how many hours you are with your family.

We did not fight this hard for the life we longed for to become so disconnected from ourselves in the process of getting it. Stop, and reconnect. Stop, notice your feelings and honour them. Stop, and be kind.

Over the years, I have learned as much from the brave mamas who shared their journeys with me as I've learned from the big names I have studied and interviewed. Women who have opened up to me – practically a stranger – and shared their innermost thoughts and struggles. Mamas who were ashamed that they had hit their kids out of frustration, and mamas who had beaten themselves up for years about how little they bonded with their babies when they first arrived.

But over the time we spend together, something starts to change. There's a spark of realisation that it all begins with them – the love, the forgiveness, the happiness, the mindfulness. Just as this mama discovered in her own 'aha' moment:

Nobody ever listened to me – I wasn't listening to myself.

I struggled to make lasting connections with people – I was disconnected from myself.

I didn't feel appreciated – I put myself at the bottom of my list.

I felt alone and unsupported – I was my own worst critic.

Our relationship with ourselves is what must come first if we are to be happy. The connection depletion has to end. Our children are watching – and we don't want them to learn that the only way to love someone is to sacrifice yourself and your wellbeing. We don't want them to see that stress is the norm, and that disconnection from our spirits is our definition of success.

One day, we will look back at this time of our lives – the time when we were figuring out how to stay sane while juggling it all – and we'll marvel at what we did. But I don't want to wish I did it differently. I don't want to miss this time and screw up my health again. What I do want is to create a new definition of success for my daughters, one that shows them a woman can be both creative and driven, soft and hard, passionate and compassionate. That's what our generation of mothers is doing: we're redefining what it means to be a woman. And it starts with us.

'It is time to get started. It is time to wake up. Don't wait another minute. Claim your heart, and claim your glory. You have all you need. Bless other women. Do not tear them down. Remember they are you – your sisters, teachers, mothers, daughters. And then look on men with the eyes the goddess gives you, and hold on. The new world will seem like nothing you have seen before. It will be reborn like you. It will shine like you. It will smile like you. It will feel like home ...'

Marianne Williamson, A Woman's Worth

Acknowledgements

I have always loved the acknowledgements at the back of a book. I would read every heartfelt sentence, hoping deep in my soul that I would get to write my own one day. So please forgive me for gushing – this has been a long time coming.

None of this would have ever happened if it weren't for my husband, Marque. The man who saw the feisty, ambitious and determined-to-be-single girl in a cocktail bar all those years ago and thought *that's the one*. You saw something in me I didn't see in myself for many years. The life and family we've created is a dream come true. Thank you.

There are a number of women who have been my support and my shoulder to cry on. Eliza, Kate, Jess, Shelley, Robyn, Andrina, Wyleng – what would I have done without your guidance (and those afternoons of much-needed bubbles)? Mel, like Marque, you've always seen more in me, and your support while I went to New York to pursue my dreams was freaking amazing. To raise a family and be a strong woman you need like-minded soul sisters around you, and I've always had that with you all.

Three key women have steered me towards this path: Tara Bliss, Julie Parker and Belinda Davidson. Each of you came into my life at the perfect time to show me that there was a different way. I am certain that I wouldn't be here without your belief in me or your wisdom and vision. Thank you for changing my life's direction.

To the amazing mamas who put their trust in a complete stranger, signed up for my program and shared their lives with me, thank you. My 'original' Reconnect Mamas – you know who you are – you have made this book possible

To my sister and confidante, I will never forget how you came to my side when Scarlett was born, spending hours helping me learn to breastfeed, sitting on my bed and bringing laughter into my house again. You got me through the toughest times, and you still do. To my amazing mum and dad – you always knew I would write a book, and your faith in me has held me high when I couldn't do it myself. I hope I have the same influence on my children's lives as you both have had on mine.

Thank you to Affirm Press for believing in me right from the beginning, and supporting me to write the book I longed to put out into the world. Seriously, a writer's dream come true. To Grace Breen for sensing I might have something to say, and to Ruby Ashby-Orr for making writing and then editing a book on the world's tightest deadline actually enjoyable.

Thank you also to each of the amazing interviewees in this book: Sarah Napthali, Therese Kerr, Julia Jones, Antonia Kidman, Nadine Richardson and Grace Gedeon. I am so grateful for your knowledge, support and willingness to share your insights so other mamas can begin their own reconnection journey.

And finally, to my babies. Scarlett, Greta and Cass – you are my greatest teachers. Thank you for choosing me as your mummy, and for showing me what love really is. Each of you has taught me so much, and you continue to make me want to be a better person, every single day. Love you to the moon and back again. X